Ultimum Mysterium

Beyond the Cutting Edge of Science

Ultimum Mysterium

Beyond the Cutting Edge of Science

Anthony Burns

Winchester, UK
Washington, USA

First published by Sixth Books, 2016
Sixth Books is an imprint of John Hunt Publishing Ltd., Laurel House, Station Approach,
Alresford, Hants, SO24 9JH, UK
office1@jhpbooks.net
www.johnhuntpublishing.com
www.6th-books.com

For distributor details and how to order please visit the 'Ordering' section on our website.

Text copyright: Anthony Burns 2015

ISBN: 978 1 78535 260 7
Library of Congress Control Number: 2015954378

A CIP catalogue record for this book is available from the British Library.

Design: Stuart Davies

Printed in the USA by Edwards Brothers Malloy

We operate a distinctive and ethical publishing philosophy in all
areas of our business, from our global network of authors to
production and worldwide distribution.

CONTENTS

Introduction   1

I: The Puzzle   5

1:   A Bizarre World   6
2:   Even Scientists Dream   44
3:   Does Astrology Work?   56
4:   The Scientists Investigate   65

II: The Physics   75

5:   What is Time?   76
6:   The Pixellated Universe   90
7:   Brains, Computers and Consciousness   101
8:   Rule by Mathematics   115
9:   Science at the Crossroads   128

III: The Philosophy   137

10: Philosophy and Science   138
11: Limits to the Imagination   145
12: Building a Universe   152
13: The Physics of Astrology   159
14: The Making of Man   167

Postscript   174

Further Reading   176

Index   183

To all my friends at Jenny's Sanctuary

Introduction

Impossible things happen. They ought not to, but they do. We like to think that we live in a stable, well-ordered universe whose laws we are able to discover and understand. And, for the most part, this is true. But time and again, people from all over the world and from all walks of life have reported strange events – apparent glitches in reality – which simply 'ought not' to happen. Such phenomena seemingly contradict the laws of physics and common sense. Nevertheless such occurrences *do* happen. If only one person reports an anomaly in the workings of things, we may say that the person is deluded, fantasizing, even hallucinating, and it is common to take this view. However, if several people observe the same anomaly (or a similar one), we may take this as an indication that our preconceptions about the workings of nature are wrong, and that we need to reconsider our theories on how the universe works.

Many centuries ago, we knew very little about the workings of nature. We thought that the surface of the earth was flat and that 'up' was the same direction everywhere. Also, in our ignorance, we thought that thunderstorms, earthquakes, volcanic eruptions and eclipses of the sun and moon were all the work of angry, capricious gods who needed to be appeased through ritual and sacrifice. We now know better than this, of course. There are no 'angry gods' out there. The earth is a rocky sphere orbiting the sun, and earthquakes, eclipses and the like are simply part of the normal workings of nature.

The quest to understand the world in which we live has been a long and difficult one. Historically, there have been three fairly distinct approaches which, for brevity, we might label the Shamanic, Scriptural and Scientific approaches – although there is, most likely, some overlap between the first two of these.

The Shamanic phase probably arose from the belief that

natural disasters and the like were perpetrated by angry gods who could nonetheless be appeased through ritual and sacrifice. Our ancestors were, of course, meticulous observers of the heavens and of birds and animals, and their rituals would have been developed on an *ad hoc* basis, evolving over time through trial and error. Sometimes their methods appeared to work; sometimes they did not. In any case, many of the belief systems underlying the Shamanic approach have survived into modern times and are widely extant even in industrialized communities, having enjoyed a significant revival in the 1960s. The practices of divination and astrology are essentially part of this tradition, as are the practices of druidry, paganism and witchcraft. And it appears – at least in some instances – that the Shamanic approach does actually work. I have heard, for example, that African witch-doctors have a higher success rate at treating snakebite than the hospitals do. Despite the apparent mumbo-jumbo, it is evident that the Shamanic tradition (and I apply this term liberally) is rich in ancient, practical wisdom which we would be foolish to reject.

The Scriptural approach (which may also be referred to as the Orthodox Religious approach) relies heavily on written records of historical events, edicts and philosophy which have been preserved down the centuries. These are often believed to emanate directly from God, and are generally accepted as dogma. I cannot and will not say which, if any, of the scriptures and their interpretations is 'right'. This issue has long been a contentious one, and I make no judgement, except to say that it is unfortunate that there has been – and still is – so much disagreement among the followers of different creeds. Much of what is written in the scriptures is, no doubt, of great value and ought to be preserved. But none of the scriptures gives a clear explanation of natural phenomena or of how the universe actually 'works'.

By far the greatest advances in our understanding of the universe have come through the Scientific approach. Although the ancient Greeks conducted their own studies, the Scientific phase did not begin in earnest until around the time of Galileo, when he made astronomical observations using a telescope. The Scientific approach involves setting up experiments, either to make general observations or to test a hypothesis. It is most important, in this respect, that any experiments are *repeatable*, so that any observations made can be either confirmed or refuted by independent observers.

The scientific advances made in the twentieth century, in particular, have been staggering and, especially in physics, have yielded results that most people find quite implausible. This has been particularly true in the fields of relativity and quantum mechanics, which we shall look at in detail later in this book. We must realize, however, that the 'impossible' is only deemed so because it contradicts at least some of the assumptions we have already made regarding the nature of things.

In the absence of concrete evidence we all have a tendency to speculate and to form our own hypotheses on how things 'ought' to be. This is how belief systems arise. Also, it must never be forgotten that scientific theories are themselves systems of belief, just as much as religious faiths are. But in any case, whether our stance is a religious or a scientific one, we are generally quite shocked if we find evidence that contradicts our cherished belief system.

People who follow the Scriptural approach often have very firm views on how things are, and generally cannot be persuaded to think otherwise, however strong the evidence. On the other hand, people who embrace the Shamanic traditions (in modern times, at least) tend to be much more flexible in their approach and are open to new ideas. Scientists are somewhere between these extremes. They like to think of themselves as being open and flexible, but this is not always the case. Even Albert Einstein was shocked when he learnt that the elementary 'particles' that compose matter are, like light, waves as well as particles.

In Section I of this book we shall examine a number of reportedly true cases, both from history and from more recent times, which are so bizarre that even current scientific theories are unable to offer an explanation. Indeed, the majority of scientists refuse to accept such reports as genuine, and so ignore the subject altogether. They dismiss such reports as fanciful and impossible. But the impossible happens, anyway. It is only because of our previous – often cherished – assumptions that we deem certain kinds of events to be impossible.

In Section II we shall review the latest scientific discoveries (mainly in physics, but also in neurological research) with a view to seeing whether these can yet offer any kind of explanation to the strange phenomena described in Section I. Then, in Section III we shall examine the underlying philosophical issues to see what may be possible in terms of a scientific explanation. The universe is what it is, regardless of what we may think about its workings. If the impossible happens, so be it. We need keep an open mind on the subject. Welcome to the bizarre, but fascinating, world of the impossible.

Anthony Burns
September 2015

I : The Puzzle

1: A Bizarre World

Prehistoric man hardly understood the workings of nature at all. No one knew what the stars were, or the moon, or the sun. Thunderstorms, earthquakes, volcanic activity and eclipses of the sun or moon were all perceived as supernatural events, perpetrated by angry and capricious gods. Virtually all natural phenomena were seen as inexplicable and therefore miraculous. But over the years – and the centuries – a few intrepid souls took it upon themselves to start investigating the phenomena in a systematic way to find out what was really going on.

One of the earliest pioneers was Pliny the Elder who boldly sailed across the Bay of Naples to observe the eruption of Mount Vesuvius in AD 79 – an exploit which was to cost him his life. Later investigators included Galileo, who built telescopes to observe the moon and planets, and Sir Isaac Newton who demonstrated that white light was a mixture of colours, as well as formulating his famous law of gravity. Benjamin Franklin demonstrated the electrical nature of thunderstorms by flying a kite with a wire attached. He found that he got an electric spark when he touched a key which he had fastened to the end of the wire. And, in the early twentieth century, Alfred Wegener proposed the theory of continental drift in which he suggested that convection currents in the earth's mantle moved the continents around – an idea which was initially rejected by scientists until the evidence provided by rock strata, fossils and magnetic field reversals confirmed this theory. Today, plate tectonics is mainstream geological science, explaining once and for all the reasons for seismic and volcanic activity. Little by little, the mysteries of nature have been unravelled until today, what were once regarded as 'supernatural' events are now seen for what they are – natural occurrences that follow definite laws. The 'capricious gods' of yesteryear have disappeared, to be replaced by a new scientific understanding.

Or have they?

Even as I write, in the early part of the twenty-first century, there is yet a substantial body of reported phenomena which seem to defy all attempts at any kind of scientific explanation. These are mostly of a subjective nature, and are often dismissed by scientists as hoaxes or figments of the human imagination.

Scientific knowledge is built up by proposing hypotheses which are then tested through a series of repeatable experiments. If the experimental results appear to favour a particular hypothesis, this then becomes accepted by scientists as mainstream theory. But no theory is ever conclusively 'proved' by experimental results: it can only be disproved. Acceptance of any scientific theory is thus always provisional.

When it comes to investigating so-called 'paranormal' phenomena, however, scientists have long been challenged to devise repeatable experiments which could, once and for all, confirm or refute any such reports. Many still do not believe such phenomena to be genuine, and so refuse to consider the issue at all. Not all scientists have taken such a cynical view, however, and systematic research on the paranormal has successfully been carried out on numerous occasions. We shall examine details of this research in Chapter 4.

We must remember that hoaxes have long been rife in this area, the case of the Cottingley Fairies being a classical example. Early in the twentieth century, a pair of young girls cut out some pictures of fashion models from a magazine and photographed them in their parents' garden at Cottingley, near Bradford, Yorkshire. They then passed these off as genuine photographs of 'fairies' which they claimed to have seen in the garden. For several decades, even the scientific experts of the day were duped by the pictures. It was only when she was in her seventies that one of the perpetrators finally owned up to what she and her companion had done all those years ago.

Sometimes the application of a little common sense is all that is needed to explain away a spooky story. A particularly ghoulish tale concerns Hagberry Pot, a small, but very deep pool in the River Ythan (the name rhymes with 'python') in Aberdeenshire, Scotland. In 1644, the Laird of the nearby Gight Castle commissioned two divers to retrieve some treasure which he had previously dumped in the pool to prevent it from being pillaged. One of the divers disappeared and was never seen again; the other re-emerged from the pool in a state of abject terror, saying that the Devil was down there, surrounded by a lot of serpents. Despite the diver's protestations, the Laird coerced him into going down once more into the pool, to fetch the treasure. A few minutes later, however, the diver's dismembered body floated back to the surface of the pool.

So what *really* happened at Hagberry Pot, that day? We can safely dismiss any reference to the Devil; this was almost certainly a product of the poor man's fevered imagination. And the serpents? The Ythan, like other rivers in the area, is a renowned fishing river, notably for salmon, trout – and *pike*. Pike fish have long, eel-like bodies and powerful jaws with sharp teeth; they can grow quite large and are notoriously aggressive. This leaves little doubt as to what must have happened to the two divers: they were attacked by shoals of hungry pike. Mystery solved.

Not all mysteries are as easily explained as this, however. There is a substantial body of well-documented cases, much of it historical, but some more recent, for which no rational explanation has ever been forthcoming. These cases are not hoaxes, but even modern scientific theories cannot explain them. There is insufficient space in this book to give an exhaustive account of all such cases, but it is worthwhile recounting a broad selection of typical examples. The remainder of the chapter is devoted to this. Several of the cases referred to are fairly well known, others less so. The one thing they do all have in common, though, is that they are *unexplained*. The first such case is from the same historical period as the Hagberry Pot incident.

Case 1: The Battle of Edgehill (1642)

The Battle of Edgehill took place on 23rd October 1642. It was the first major battle of the English Civil War, and resulted in a defeat for the Royalists. The story of the battle didn't end there, however. A pamphlet published three months later (in January 1643) contained the following quotation:

> *Between twelve and one of the clock in the morning was heard by some shepherds, and other country-men, and travellers, first the sound of drummes afar off, and the noyse of souldiers, as it were, giving out their last groanes; at which they were much amazed... But then, on the sudden ... appeared in the ayre those same incorporeall souldiers that made those clamours, and immediately, with Ensignes display'd, Drummes beating, Musquets going off, Cannons discharged, horses neyghing (which also to these men were visible), the alarum or entrance to this game of death was struck up... Till two or three in the morning, in equal scale continued this dreadful fight ... so amazing and terrifying the poore men, that they could not give credit to their ears and eyes; run away they durst not, for feare of being made a prey to these infernall souldiers, and so they, with much feare and affright, stayed to behold the outcome of the business.*

(Quoted from *The Penguin Book of Ghosts* by Westwood & Simpson)

Those who had witnessed this terrifying vision reported it to a magistrate and a clergyman, swearing that it was true. In the nights following, many people gathered to see if anything would happen, and they saw exactly these same sights. Reports reached the King (Charles I) who sent six 'reliable officers' to investigate the story. Not only did the officers take sworn witness statements, but they saw for themselves the vision in the sky. They even recognized several of their colleagues who they knew had died in the battle. On their return, they reported all of this to the King on oath.

Similar visions were later reported from Naseby, Northamptonshire, following the battle there in 1645.

Today the road from Banbury to Kineton crosses a small part of the Edgehill battlefield, but the greater part of the site is now owned by the Ministry of Defence, and is closed to the public. There have been no reports of similar sightings in recent times. However, a small monument to the battle stands at the roadside near Kineton.

Evidently something extraordinary *did* happen, both at Edgehill and later at Naseby, following the battles there. The fact that so many people witnessed these events strongly suggests that some underlying physical principle was at work about which we know nothing – but which suggests that there must be something very peculiar about the nature of time.

Here is another well-documented case, this time from the beginning of the twentieth century:

Case 2: *The Palace of Versailles*

This case was reported independently to the eminent scientist, Professor Sir WF Barrett FRS by two schoolteachers from Oxford, Miss Anne Moberley and Miss Eleanor Frances Jourdain, regarding their visit to the Palace of Versailles in August, 1901.

Their extraordinary experience evidently began when they noted a 'very sweet air' circulating through the famous Hall of Mirrors where they were sitting. They left the building, walked down to the end of the Grand Canal and then turned right, where they followed one of the many woodland footpaths there. They observed that the weather had become overcast, although it had been sunny and bright that morning. Coming to the Petit Canal, not far from the Grand Trianon, they recognized the latter and tried using it as a landmark to get their bearings. Passing it on the left, they came to what they described as 'a broad green drive, perfectly deserted'. They crossed the drive and, turning to the right, saw some buildings. Miss Moberley reported seeing a woman shaking a white cloth from an upstairs window, but her friend evidently did not. Further ahead, the path divided into three, and the ladies saw two men on the central path. At first, they thought these men were gardeners because a spade and a wheelbarrow were standing close by; but the men were wearing tricorn hats and long green coats, which seemed rather strange. It became evident that these men were not gardeners after all. The two directed the ladies (by a hand gesture?) to continue along the central path.

At this point, Miss Moberley felt an unaccountable sense of sadness and depression, but did not mention this to her friend, as she did not wish to spoil the visit for her. (Miss Jourdain later reported having had a similar feeling at this point.) To the left, they caught sight of a sinister-looking man sitting beside what they described as 'a light garden kiosk'. He was wearing a cloak and a wide-brimmed hat, and had a hideously pockmarked face. The trees behind him looked somewhat unreal, similar to trees in a tapestry.

A second man suddenly emerged, seemingly from nowhere, forcefully urging them to take the path straight ahead, which they did. Like the pockmarked man, this man also wore a cloak. He vanished as abruptly as he had appeared, although the sound of running footsteps persisted for some time afterward. The two ladies continued along the path, crossing a small bridge over a miniature ravine. Their route took them through part of the forest and then alongside a meadow with long grass, which gave an impression of greyness and wetness. Further ahead, Miss Moberley (but not Miss Jourdain) caught sight of a lady sitting at an easel, sketching. The lady was wearing a light summer dress and a wide-brimmed hat. Miss Moberley described the lady's features as pretty, but not young.

Some time after their visit to Versailles, Miss Moberley saw a painting of Marie Antoinette with her two children, and immediately recognized her as the lady she had seen sketching at the easel.

Was this case a time slip? Or was it, as Professor Barrett insisted, a 'remarkable collective hallucination'? I offer no answer to this, but the next case also bears the hallmarks of a possible 'collective hallucination'.

Case 3: The Phantom Guest House

This case involves a Mr and Mrs Clifford Pye who were on holiday in Cornwall in 1933. They were travelling by bus from Wadebridge to the coastal village of Boscastle, where they intended to find a guest house. Just before the road drops down into the village, the bus stopped to set down a passenger. At this point Mr Pye noticed a large house on the left-hand side of the road, which he thought looked eminently suitable. He writes:

It [the bus] had come to rest almost outside the gates of a rather substantial house, standing on the left-hand side of the road. It stood back from the road some twenty yards or so, there being a semi-circular drive from the gate outside where we had stopped to another gate twenty-five yards further on. The garden front was screened from the road by a hedge over which we could just see from our seats in the bus. The house was double-fronted, and of a style of architecture which I judged to be from the late 1860s or early 1870s. It had a fresh, trim appearance, and seemed to have been recently painted, the woodwork and quoins of the house being of a rather reddish, light chocolate colour. The most striking feature, however, was on the lawn, where, among beds of scarlet geraniums, there were several wicker and cane chairs and tables over which were standing large garden umbrellas of black and orange. No person was seen, nor do I recollect having seen any sign notifying that it was a guest-

house, though I had no doubt that such was the case. I called my wife's attention to the place and she immediately replied that it was 'just what we are looking for' but, before we could come to any decision, the bus moved off and in two or three minutes we were down in Boscastle.

(From *The Personality of Man* by GNM Tyrrell, p 65)

Mr and Mrs Pye were not greatly attracted to Boscastle and so, while Mr Pye stayed to look after the luggage, Mrs Pye set off back to the guest house which they had just seen. An hour and a half later, Mrs Pye returned, looking tired and frustrated, saying that she could not find the guest house, and that she had booked a room at a different one in Trevalga, about a mile further up the road. As they travelled back, by bus, Mr Pye thought he knew where the original guest house was; but when they looked again, it wasn't there. All they saw was an expanse of open fields.

The proprietor of the Trevalga guest house later told them that there was no house anywhere in the area resembling the one they had reported seeing.

In her book *Time Storms*, the author Jenny Randles gives numerous examples of apparent time slips. The next three cases are taken from her book, the first of which is an interesting case bearing resonances with the previous one.

Case 4: Montélimar, France

In October 1979, the Simpson and Gisby families from Kent went on holiday together to Spain, driving there through France. Seeking accommodation for the night, they drove along a back road near the town of Montélimar. They noticed that there was no other traffic on that road, and that it seemed suspiciously quiet. They came to a small hotel where they checked in for the night, but it looked strangely antiquated and the staff wore old-fashioned clothes. Next morning, when they paid the bill, it turned out to be ridiculously cheap. And a policeman, of whom they asked directions, had evidently never heard of motorways.

On the return leg of the trip, the two families decided that they would use the same hotel again for their overnight stay. They found the road again, but the hotel was not there! Photographs of the hotel, which they had taken on their first visit, were missing from the film when it was developed.

Case 5: The Road to Bedford

In September 1973, a young Bedfordshire man was driving home from the village of Little Houghton, Northamptonshire, in the early hours of the morning. As he had a long journey ahead of him, he had had very little to drink. He noted the time of 2 a.m. on the church clock, as he drove past, but recalled nothing more until, some five hours later, he found himself wandering around Bromham, Bedfordshire, on foot. The car was nowhere to be seen. Although uninjured, he presumed that he must have had an accident with the car, and had carried on walking.

He managed to contact a friend, who drove him back along the road to look for the car, eventually sighting it in the middle of a muddy field near Turville. *But there were no tyre tracks in the mud, and the gate was shut.* On examination, they found the car locked, and the young man realized that the car keys were in his pocket. The field was too muddy for the car to be driven out, and the farmer had to tow it out for them with his tractor.

Two years later, the young man suddenly recalled that he had seen a fuzzy white light ahead of him as he passed the church, but had been aware of nothing more until he found himself wandering around Bromham.

Case 6: A Missed Meeting

Another case, not unlike the previous one, involved a company representative, Jorge Ramos of Linhares, Brazil. On 20th April 1981, he set off from home at 6.30 p.m. to attend a business meeting. Although his destination was only a few miles away, however, he never arrived. His abandoned car was found the next day, with the key still in the ignition. All of his papers, files and demonstration materials were still in the car and intact. It thus appeared that Mr Ramos had been abducted.

Five days later, in a distressed state, he telephoned his wife. He told her that, while driving to his meeting, he had seen a white glow ahead of him, which had enveloped the car. He had then found himself apparently floating in a dreamy state. He was now some 600 miles from where the car had been found, unaware that five days had passed.

The cases described thus far have featured apparent dislocations in both time and space, as experienced by the subjects. The next few cases, again well documented, suggest that it is sometimes possible to foresee future events, often – but not always – through dreams. I begin with two fairly well known cases:

Case 7: Abraham Lincoln's Prophetic Dream
During the American Civil War, Abraham Lincoln, who was the then President, reported the following dream to his wife and to his friend, Ward Lamon:

About ten days ago, I retired very late. I had been up waiting for important dispatches from the front. I could not have been long in bed when I fell into a slumber, for I was weary. I soon began to dream. There seemed to be a death-like stillness about me. Then I heard subdued sobs, as if a number of people were weeping. I thought I left my bed and went downstairs. There the silence was broken by the same pitiful sobs, but the mourners were invisible. I went from room to room; no living person was in sight, but the mournful sounds of distress met me as I passed along. I saw light in all the rooms; every object was familiar to me; but where were all the people who were grieving as if their hearts would break? I was

15

puzzled and alarmed. What could be the meaning of all this? Determined to find the cause of a state of things so mysterious and so shocking, I kept on until I arrived at the East Room, which I entered. There I met a sickening surprise. Before me was a catafalque, on which rested a corpse in funeral vestments. Around it were stationed soldiers who were acting as guards; and there was a throng of people, gazing mournfully on the corpse, whose face was covered, others weeping pitifully. 'Who is dead in the White House?' I demanded of one of the soldiers. 'The President,' was his answer; 'he was killed by an assassin.' Then came a loud burst of grief from the crowd, which woke me from my dream. I slept no more that night; and although it was only a dream, I have been strangely annoyed by it ever since.'

(Transcribed from *Science and Psychic Phenomena* by Chris Carter; original quote from *Recollections of Abraham Lincoln 1847–1865* by Ward Lamon, pp 116–117)

Three days after recounting his dream, Abraham Lincoln was assassinated in Ford's Theatre, and his body subsequently lay in state in the East Room of the White House.

It is known also that Ulysses S Grant and his wife were scheduled to accompany the President to Ford's Theatre, that night, and to sit with him in his balcony box. But Mrs Grant also had a strong premonition that something would happen and, despite the urgency of her husband's business, persuaded him to forgo the theatre visit and to return home with her to New Jersey.

Case 8: Morgan Robertson and the Titanic

Here, we have another case of apparently seeing into the future, this time through the medium of a novel, written a full fourteen years before the presaged event. The novel was entitled *Futility* and featured a luxury liner, uncannily named *Titan*, which was deemed unsinkable, but which was struck by an iceberg and sank with a heavy loss of life. The *Titanic* sank in identical circumstances in April, 1912. There are numerous points of similarity between the novel and the actual event, as listed here:

- The ship in the story was called *Titan*; the real one was called *Titanic*.
- Both ships were luxury liners.
- Both ships were on their maiden voyage from England to the USA.
- The *Titan* was described as being 800 feet long; the *Titanic* was 882 feet long.
- Both ships had a carrying capacity of some 3,000 passengers.
- Both ships were driven by three screw propellers.
- Both ships were deemed unsinkable because of their design.
- The *Titan* had 19 watertight compartments, separated by bulkheads; the *Titanic* had 16 such bulkheads.
- The *Titan* had only twenty-four lifeboats; the *Titanic* had only twenty.
- Both ships sailed in April.
- Both ships were struck on the starboard side by an iceberg.
- Both ships sank with a heavy loss of life.

The string of coincidences here strongly suggests an element of causality. Yet another (less well-known) case of apparent foreknowledge concerns a plane crash at Chicago's O'Hare Airport in 1979:

Case 9: Flight 191

In 1979, David Booth of Cincinatti had the same recurring nightmare every night between 15th and 24th May of that year. He repeatedly dreamt that a passenger airliner was coming in to land, but that it did not make the usual amount of noise as it did so. Suddenly, the plane banked to the right, turned upside down and crashed nose first. By 24th May, Mr Booth was so distraught that he contacted Cincinatti Airport, giving details of his dream to Paul Williams of the Federal Aviation Administration.

The next day, American Airlines Flight 191 was approaching Chicago's O'Hare Airport, and had been given permission to land. Suddenly, it banked to the right, turned upside down and crashed nose first – exactly as in David Booth's dream.

Case 10: J W Dunne and his Experiments

Around the turn of the 20th century, the author J W Dunne had a series of premonitory dreams, the most spectacular of which presaged the eruption of Mont Pelée, on the island of Martinique, in the spring of 1902. He writes:

I seemed to be standing on high ground – the upper slopes of some spur of a hill or mountain. The ground was of a curious white formation. Here and there in this were little fissures, and from these jets of vapour were spouting upward. In my dream I recognized the place as an island of which I had dreamed before – an island which was in imminent peril from a volcano. And, when I saw the vapour spouting from the ground, I gasped: 'It's the island! Good Lord, the whole thing is going to blow up!' For I had memories of reading about Krakatoa, where the sea, making its way into the heart of the volcano through a submarine crevice, flashed into steam, and blew the whole mountain to pieces. Forthwith I was seized with a frantic desire to save the four thousand (I knew the number) unsuspecting inhabitants. Obviously there was only one way of doing this, and that was to take them off in ships. There followed a most distressing nightmare, in which I was at a neighbouring island, trying to get the incredulous French authorities to despatch vessels of every and any description to remove the inhabitants of the threatened island. I was sent from one official to another; and finally woke myself by my own dream exertions, clinging to the heads of a team of horses drawing the carriage of one 'Monsieur le Maire', who was going out to dine

and wanted me to return when his office would be open the next day.
All through the dream the number of people in danger obsessed my
mind. I repeated it to every one I met, and, at the moment of waking,
I was shouting to the 'Maire', 'Listen! Four thousand people will be
killed unless —

(From *An Experiment with Time* by J W Dunne, pp 21–22)

At the time of the dream, Dunne was encamped at Lindley in the
then Orange Free State. When he next received a batch of
newspapers from Britain, the centre spread of the *Daily Telegraph*
caught his attention. It read:

VOLCANO DISASTER

IN

MARTINIQUE

TOWN SWEPT AWAY

AN AVALANCHE OF FLAME

PROBABLE LOSS OF OVER

40,000 LIVES

BRITISH STEAMER BURNT

The town in question was St Pierre, the capital of the island of
Martinique. Because of his dream, Dunne initially read the death
toll as 4,000. Only at a later date did he realize that the figure was
ten times this number.

Dreams such as this one spurred Dunne to carry out a series
of experiments in which he enlisted a number of volunteers to
keep dream diaries. He then tried to correlate the dream contents
thus recorded with actual waking events occurring subsequently.
He was particularly on the lookout for *unusual* dream events
being borne out later in real life. He noted the time intervals
between the dreams and any similar waking events occurring in
the days following, trying to estimate the *probability* of such
events occurring so soon after the dream itself.

The results were, predictably, somewhat mixed, with several subjects hardly producing any worthwhile results at all. Some subjects, however, produced a significant number of 'hits'. In one particularly interesting case, the subject dreamed about an unusual punt-like boat constructed from old cartwheels cut in half. (Dunne included a drawing of the boat in his book.) The dreamer actually saw a boat very similar to the one in the dream, about a month later.

Dunne gave much thought on these matters and the possible implications regarding the nature of time itself. I shall be returning to this subject in a later chapter; but essentially his idea was that time consisted of more than one dimension – possibly an infinite number – in which each additional dimension provided a measure against which the previous one could be scaled.

Case 11: A Long-Term Prophecy?

As this is not a religious book as such, I am somewhat hesitant to include a case taken from the Old Testament. In Chapter 7 of the Book of Daniel, however, the prophet describes a dream in which he saw four terrifying creatures which, he was told, symbolized four 'great kingdoms' which would come to dominate the earth. Alternative interpretations have been mooted, but the symbolism of the four creatures does appear to bear strong resonances with contemporary geopolitical scene.

The creatures thus described are: i) a lion with eagle's wings; ii) a bear; iii) a leopard with fowl's wings; iv) an extremely powerful and destructive beast which 'devoured, broke in pieces and stamped on the residue with its feet'. The first three creatures appear, on the face of it, to correspond respectively to: i) Britain and the United States of America; ii) Russia; and iii) Continental Europe (which could be interpreted as either Nazi Germany or the European Union). I make no comment about the fourth creature.

If this interpretation of the symbolism is indeed correct, then this is an extraordinary case of long-range precognition, spanning a period of more than two thousand years.

Remote Viewing and Out-of-Body Experiences

Seeing beyond the physical can entail not only seeing ahead in time, but also viewing scenes at distant locations where the observer is not physically present. This is usually known as 'remote viewing', but is also sometimes referred to as 'travelling clairvoyance'. Some people simply 'see' something in their mind's eye that is really elsewhere – but others have a sensation of leaving their physical bodies and actually visiting the places they have seen. The next case refers to an individual who has often viewed remote scenes – and with spectacular results:

Case 12: Ingo Swann

Ingo Douglas Swann first had an out-of-body experience during surgery at the age of two. He was somewhat unsettled by the sight of the operation and, on waking from the anaesthetic, he asked for his tonsils back. The nurse told him, however, that they had been thrown away. He said that this was not true and that the surgeon had put them in a bottle and placed them behind some rolls of tissue – which subsequently turned out to be the case.

His early years were otherwise uneventful, but in adult life, after some eleven years in an army career, he became interested in psychical research and was willing to have his own skills tested. He took part in a series of experiments, conducted by Russell Targ and Harold Puthoff, in which he was given the co-ordinates (longitude and latitude) of various locations around the world, and asked to describe anything he could see there by remote viewing. His abilities turned out to be impressive. In one example, he was given the co-ordinates of a location on the east coast of the USA. His description ran thus:

This seems to be some sort of mounds or rolling hills. There is a city in the north; I can see tall buildings and some smog. This seems to be a strange place, somewhat like the lawns that one would find around a military base, but I get the impression that there are either some old bunkers around, or maybe a covered reservoir. There must be a flagpole, some highways to the west, possibly a river over to the east, to the south more city.

(Transcribed from *The Out-of-Body Experience* by Anthony Peake, pp 82–83; original quote from *Mind Reach* by Russell Targ and Harold Puthoff, p2)

Swann went on to draw a map of the area he had seen, which turned out to be remarkably accurate, not only in the details but also in the scaling and distances. Results such as this were of such high quality that Targ and Puthoff were awarded funding for a three-year research programme.

Then, in 1973, as the NASA space probe was approaching the planet Jupiter, Swann and another subject, Harold Sherman, were asked to report what, if anything, they could see of the planet by remote viewing. For the duration of the experiment, Swann and Sherman sat in locations some 2,000 miles apart, making connivance impossible. Swann reported:

Very high in the atmosphere there are crystals, they glitter. Maybe the stripes are like bands of crystals, maybe like the rings of Saturn, though not far out like that. Very close within the atmosphere. I bet you they'll reflect radio probes. Is that possible if you had a cloud of crystals that were assaulted by radio waves?

There is an enormous range about 31,000 feet high. The mountains are huge.

Sherman independently reported:

There appear to be huge volcanic peaks, great cones rising some miles.

(Both quotes transcribed from *The Out-of-Body Experience* by Anthony Peake, pp 84–85; original texts from *Mind Reach* by Russell Targ and Harold Puthoff, pp 208 and 210)

At first, these did not sound like very accurate descriptions of the planet Jupiter. The planet itself is a gas giant, probably lacking a solid core, and common sense says that there could not be any mountains there. However, the satellite Io, quite surprisingly at the time, was found to be covered with numerous volcanoes. Also, some six years later, when the probe *Voyager 1* reached Jupiter, it confirmed the presence of a faint ring, similar to the ones around Saturn, but much narrower and closer to the surface of the planet.

Out-of-body experiences were known as long ago as the time of the ancient Egyptians. There is much literature on the subject, but the salient feature of this experience is of finding oneself inhabiting a duplicate body, made of some rarefied material and located outside the 'physical' one, sometimes connected to it by a fine, silvery thread. The consistency of such reports from various sources suggests that this is a real phenomenon. Many of the experiences of Sylvan Muldoon and Robert Monroe, in particular, were vivid and spectacular (if somewhat alarming) and are worth recounting here.

Case 13: Sylvan Muldoon

Sylvan Joseph Muldoon (1903–71) had many out-of-body experiences during his lifetime, and wrote extensively about them. His first such episode was at the age of twelve, not long after his mother had taken him and his younger brother on a visit to a Spiritualist centre at Clinton, Iowa. (His mother had been inquisitive about spirit phenomena, hence the visit.) He writes:

I dozed off to sleep about ten-thirty o'clock, in the same natural manner as I had always done before, and slept for several hours. At length I realized that I was slowly awakening, yet I could not seem to drift back into slumber nor further arouse. In this bewildering stupor I knew (within me) that I existed somewhere, somehow, in a powerless, silent, dark and feelingless condition.

Still I was conscious – a very unpleasant contemplation of being! I repeat again: I was aware that I existed, but where I could not seem to understand. My memory would not tell me. The stupefaction which one experiences when first emerging from the influence of an anaesthetic is similar. I thought I was awakening from a natural sleep in a natural manner, yet I could not proceed. There was but one thing dominating my mind. Where was I? Where was I?

He mentions that, for a while, he felt *adhered* to whatever he was lying on. This was followed by a sensation of floating, but with a very strong pressure at the back of his head. He felt also that his whole body was vibrating. He began to hear far-distant sounds, but still could not move. The sense of vision quickly followed and, when he saw where he was, he was astonished to find himself floating toward the ceiling with a zigzagging motion. He was otherwise physically paralyzed and unable to move voluntarily. He continues:

I believed naturally that this was my physical body, as I had always known it, but that it had mysteriously begun to defy gravity. It was too unnatural for me to understand, yet too real to deny – for, being conscious, being able to see, I could not question my sanity. Involuntarily, at about six feet above the bed, as if the movement had been conducted by an invisible force present in the very air, I was uprighted from the horizontal position to the perpendicular, and placed standing on the floor of the room. There I stood for what seemed to me about two minutes, still powerless to move of my own accord, and staring straight ahead. I was still astrally cataleptic.

Then the controlling force relaxed. I felt free, noticing only the tension in the back of my head. I took a step, when the pressure increased for an interval and threw my body out at an acute angle. I managed to turn around. There were two of me! I was beginning to believe myself insane. There was another 'me' lying quietly upon the bed! It was difficult to convince myself that this was real, but consciousness would not allow me to doubt what I saw.

My identical bodies were joined by an elastic-like cable, one end of which was fastened to the medulla oblongata region of the astral counterpart, while the other end centred between the eyes of the physical counterpart. The cable extended across the space of probably six feet which separated us. All this time I was having difficulty keeping my balance – swaying first to one side, then to the other.

(Quotes taken from *The Projection of the Astral Body* by Sylvan J Muldoon and Hereward Carrington)

Muldoon goes on to describe how he had wandered around the house, in his 'astral' body, for around fifteen minutes, thinking that he had died. He tried to make contact with his sleeping relatives, trying to shake them, but his hands passed right through them and he became distressed. Then he felt a sharp tug at the back of the head and felt himself being pulled back, again with a zigzagging motion. He turned horizontal again, vibrating and cataleptic as before, slowly descending, then suddenly dropped back into his physical body.

On re-engaging with his physical body he felt a severe pain penetrate his whole being, as if he had been 'split open from head to foot'. Glad to be physically 'alive' once more, he was nevertheless filled with a sense of awe as he had been fully conscious throughout the whole experience.

Case 14: Robert Monroe

Robert Monroe (1915–95) was born in Lexington, Kentucky, and had worked for many years in the radio industry. One Sunday in 1958, while his family was at church, he decided to conduct an experiment on himself to investigate the effect a continuous sound might have on his concentration. Shortly after the family returned, he was troubled by an intense stomach pain, which he thought might be attributable to the experiment. The next day, the pain had gone, but he felt that something inside him had changed.

Three weeks later, again when alone on a Sunday afternoon, he was lying on the couch in his living room when he saw a beam of light shining down on him, giving his body a feeling of warmth. He knew it could not be the sun, because the light was coming from the north. His body then started shaking violently (c.f. Muldoon's 'vibrations'), and he felt unable to move. He managed to free himself from this vice-like grip, and the vibration subsided. For some reason, he felt that this was somehow connected with the stomach pain that he had experienced three weeks earlier.

This sensation visited him a further nine times over the next six weeks, always when he was at rest and dozing. By now, he was starting to become accustomed to the sensations. But then, on one occasion, he casually brushed the carpet with his hand, which had been hanging over the edge of the couch. Without at first realizing the absurdity of the situation, he felt his hand go through the carpet onto the wooden floorboards, and then through the floor into the room below. And then his fingers felt water. Suddenly realizing what was happening, he withdrew his hand and looked at it. It was dry. And there was no hole in the floor. Starting to worry about his sanity, he assumed that this had been an unpleasant dream, and discussed it with his doctor. The doctor was unable to offer an explanation, however.

A few weeks later, as he was waiting to go to sleep, he fantasized about flying a glider (he was keen on flying) and decided that he would fly one the next day. No sooner than he had had this thought, he felt a pressure on his left shoulder and, putting his hand out to ascertain what this was, he felt an unbroken surface, which he thought was the wall. But when he looked, it turned out to be the ceiling! He was able to turn round and look at the bed. He saw two people lying there: his wife – and himself.

Like Muldoon, he thought that he had died, and started to panic. At this point he swooped back down and once more found himself in the flesh.

An important difference between Muldoon's case and that of Robert Monroe is that whereas Muldoon always found himself in earthly surroundings while in the out-of-body state, Monroe visited different realms, which he termed 'locales'. One of these was, in many ways, similar to the earth – except that much of the technology was completely different. He reported, for example, trying to drive a 'car' which one propelled with one's elbows and steered with one's feet – very awkward for us earthlings!

Near-Death Experiences

Sylvan Muldoon thought that he had died when he had his first out-of-body experience, but this turned out not to be the case. For some people, however, the out-of-body trip goes further, with the subject meeting deceased loved ones and/or religious figures. They often report a sensation of travelling through a tunnel and (sometimes) undergoing a review of the life they have just lived. More often than not, they are reluctant to return to the physical body because the trip is so pleasant, and are thereafter changed by the experience.

The next case is the account of a man who hovered on the threshold between life and death for several days, as he lay in a hospital bed, suffering from typhoid fever:

Case 15: Sir Alexander Ogston

During the Boer War (1899–1902) Sir Alexander Ogston KCVO was admitted to a sanatorium, suffering from typhoid fever.

Following his recovery, he reported:

> *In my delirium, night and day made little difference to me. In the four-bedded ward where they first placed me, I lay, as it seemed, in a constant stupor, which excluded the existence of any hopes or fears. Mind and body seemed to be dual, and to some extent separate. I was conscious of the body as an inert, tumbled mass near the door; it belonged to me but it was not I. I was conscious that my mental self used regularly to leave the body...and wandered away from it under grey, sunless, moonless, starless skies, ever onwards to a distant gleam on the horizon, solitary but not unhappy...*

(From *The Personality of Man* by GNM Tyrrell, pp 199–200)

Whenever his body was disturbed in any way, Sir Alexander found himself suddenly drawn back to it, but left it again when he was once more left alone. As time passed, his wanderings through 'fields of asphodel' (as he described them) became ever more distinct until, at the height of the fever, he felt himself drawn back to the body once more and heard someone say, 'He will live.'

He went on to say that, during his wanderings, he noticed an ability to see through the walls of the building, and became aware of a poor RAMC surgeon who became very ill and died. He saw some people surreptitiously remove the body at the dead of night, and take it to a cemetery. It was later confirmed to him that this had actually happened.

In the latter half of the 20th century, Dr Raymond Moody, a specialist who has revived many cardiac arrest patients, noted how common the near-death experience is among such patients and, after collecting details of over 150 such cases, published his findings in his book *Life after Life*. His interest in the subject was first aroused when he heard of the near-death experience reported to him by Dr George Ritchie, the subject of this next case:

Case 16: Dr George Ritchie

Dr Ritchie reported to Dr Moody that in 1943 he was an army private, but was excited to learn that he had been accepted for training as a doctor at the Medical College of Virginia. However, on the eve of his enrolment at the college, he had been hospitalized with a respiratory infection. This was of great concern to him, as he was particularly anxious that he should take the train to Richmond, the next day, to attend for the enrolment. But then his temperature rose, he started to spit blood and finally blacked out. This, it seemed, was only for an instant, however.

When he opened his eyes again, he found himself in an unfamiliar room, lying in a strange bed. He assumed that the next day had already arrived and that it was time for him to go and take his train to Richmond. He jumped out of the bed, anxious to catch the train, but was astonished to see someone lying on the bed that he had just vacated. Still determined to catch his train, he ignored this oddity and walked down the corridor. He met a ward boy in the corridor, and tried to speak to him; but the boy ignored him completely and walked straight through him. Another man, a sergeant, also ignored him and seemed unaware of his presence.

He then found himself flying through the air, still wearing his hospital pyjamas. Again, people seemed unaware of his presence, and he was shocked to find that his 'body' passed through the guy-wire of a telegraph pole when he tried to lean on it. It bothered him that he would not be able to pursue a career as a doctor whilst in this peculiarly disembodied state and, realizing that his 'physical' body must still be in the hospital, decided to return to it. He went back to the hospital and, after a search, found it covered in a white sheet. At this point, he met a 'Being of Light' who told him that it was not yet his time to die. He assumed this person to be Jesus.

In an instant he woke up in his earthly body, still covered in the white sheet. This startled an orderly who was preparing to take his body to the mortuary. The orderly summoned a doctor who administered an injection of adrenaline, jolting Dr Ritchie back to life. Although having been clinically dead for nearly ten minutes, it turned out that Dr Ritchie had suffered no consequential brain damage.

Dr Moody was so intrigued by Dr Ritchie's account that it prompted him to carry out his own research into the subject. After collecting details of several more cases, and collating the results, he eventually identified nine common factors which characterized a typical near-death experience. These are:

- A sense of being dead
- Peace and painlessness
- An out-of-body experience
- A sensation of passing through a tunnel
- Being met by 'people of light'
- Rising rapidly into the heavens
- Reluctance to return to earth life
- A life review
- Meeting a 'supreme being of light'

Such cases strongly suggest that we may retain our consciousness and mental faculties beyond the demise of the physical body. If so, is there also any evidence that we had any kind of conscious awareness *before* being born into this life, and that we may have a residual memory of such an awareness?

There are numerous cases on record in which people have claimed to remember previous earthly lives – the phenomenon known as *reincarnation*. Such 'memories' are dismissed by many westerners (and most scientists) as fantasizing. However, there is evidence that some subjects have demonstrated knowledge of

1: A Bizarre World

people, places or events, which they could not possibly have obtained by ordinary means and which, when investigated, have turned out to be veridical. The following are typical cases.

Case 17: The Priest who came back

In 1972 Donna Marine, a Brazilian woman, heard her name being called, even though she was alone in the room. She immediately recognized it as the voice of Father Jonathan, a priest who had been her school chaplain many years previously, and of whom she had been particularly fond. What Donna did not know at the time was that Father Jonathan had just been killed in a road accident. When it was announced on the radio, it was reported that this had been a car accident. Donna was naturally saddened by the news.

Some eight years later, she gave birth to a baby boy whom she named Kilden Alexandre, the latter name being one that she had used informally for Father Jonathan. She gave the baby this name in memory of her late friend. The baby's early years were fairly normal except that he appeared, at times, to suffer from disturbing dreams. And then, at the age of two and a half, he started to say some strange things.

He insisted on being addressed as Alexandre, and not Kilden, asserting that he was 'the priest'. When his mother jokingly asked where he had come from, he immediately replied, 'I was on my scooter and a truck came and hit me. I fell down and banged my head, and I died.'

Shocked, his mother asked, 'When did this happen?'

'When I was padre,' he replied.

Donna immediately wrote down everything her son had told her and, puzzled by the reference to a scooter, decided to contact the police about the accident. They gave her a copy of the full report and, as it turned out, the priest had indeed been riding a scooter.

The boy recognized faces in his mother's old school photograph, and was moved to tears on hearing a song that the priest had particularly liked. Even at thirteen, his memories were still vivid.

This case was thoroughly investigated by Hernami Guimaraes Andrade, Brazil's leading psychic investigator, who was so impressed that he wrote a book about it. The book, *Renasceu Por Amor* (Reborn for Love) is available only in Portuguese, but author Guy Lyon Playfair, who knows the language, has reviewed it, and is greatly impressed by the thoroughness and objectivity of Andrade's investigation.

Case 18: The Baby with Bullet Wounds

Titu Singh was born with two prominent birthmarks on his head, which puzzled his parents at first, but which were soon forgotten when his hair grew and covered them up. However, from the age of two and a half, he started to talk of his 'other family', saying that he had owned a radio shop and that he had been killed by someone shooting him in the head. He said that his name was Suresh, and that he had a wife called Uma and two children called Ronu and Sonu.

At first his parents did not believe what he was saying but, in the end, his elder brother travelled to the nearby city of Agra (famous for the Taj Mahal) to check whether any of his little brother's claims might have any substance. He soon located a shop called Suresh Radio, and found that the woman running it was a widow by the name of Uma. She said that her husband had died from being shot in the head, and that she had two children called Ronu and Sonu. She was shocked at the suggestion that her husband had reincarnated as this young man's brother, and decided the next day to visit the family. She took with her Suresh's parents (her in-laws). On their arrival, the little boy immediately exclaimed that his 'other family' had arrived. He instantly recognized Suresh's two children from a photograph of a group of children, and amazed Uma when he asked whether she remembered an outing to a fair in a nearby town. She did remember it. Later, when given an opportunity to see the radio shop, the boy observed a number of changes that had been made to the shop since Suresh's time. And a physical examination of the boy revealed that his birthmarks were in exactly the same positions where Suresh had been shot.

Case 19: The Dalai Lama

It is well known that in Buddhist circles the Dalai Lama is believed to be the reincarnation of his predecessor. Is there any verifiable evidence that this might indeed be the case?

The thirteenth Dalai Lama died in 1933, and his body was laid in state in the Potala Palace, facing south, as is the Buddhist tradition. One morning, however, his head had mysteriously turned during the night, to face east. An oracle was consulted in which a young regent gazed into a sacred lake. In his vision he saw a three-storey monastery with gold and copper roofs, alongside of which a twisting lane lead up to a Chinese peasant-style house. The house had distinctive carved gables, painted blue. Nearby was a peach tree and a woman holding a baby in her arms. The content of this vision was written down and sealed so that it could not be tampered with.

Three groups, including monks and secular officials, then scoured the countryside to the east, the direction toward which the Dalai Lama's head had turned, taking with them a number of items that he had owned. The search eventually led to a house, which exactly matched the one seen in the vision: it was in the village of Pari Takster, not far from the Kumtum monastery. There was indeed a young boy living in the house who, on seeing the visiting dignitaries, exclaimed, 'Lama! Lama!' (The corresponding name in his own dialect was 'Aga'; he was unlikely ever to have heard the word 'Lama'.) The child grabbed the rosary that the man was wearing, saying, 'That is mine. May I have it please?' The rosary had indeed belonged to the thirteenth

Dalai Lama.

That little boy is the present (fourteenth) Dalai Lama.

Helen Wambach's Studies

The American psychologist Dr Helen Wambach (1925–85) became interested in the subject of reincarnation when she examined and reported on a possible case, but at first was not entirely convinced by it. She decided that a large-scale study was needed, using large numbers of volunteer subjects to see whether they might report any details of past lives whilst under hypnosis. She decided also that any such reports should be compared with actual historical records to see whether they tallied. In this respect she asked for details of the period in history her subjects recalled, the geographic location, the type of landscape where lived, details of dress and appearance, food and mealtimes, getting supplies, a community event, the manner of death and whether the subject recalled being male or female in that life.

She amassed a large number of positive replies and found that there was, in general, a quite good agreement with the historical records, even though, in many cases, the subjects were unfamiliar with the detailed histories of the countries and time periods involved. She found that it was common for individuals to switch gender from one incarnation to the next and that, for any given time, the genders were fairly evenly balanced. She found also that the length of the 'between-life' interval could vary from as little as a few minutes to a thousand years or more, the average being around 52 years. Interestingly, she found also that there was a tendency for whole groups of individuals to reincarnate within the same continent for approximately a thousand years, and then move on to a different continent.

Dr Wambach conducted a further study to find whether her subjects were able to recall the birth experience whilst under hypnosis. The response rate was significantly lower for this than for recalling past lives, but many subjects did respond. Again the results were quite instructive. The overall picture that emerged was that nearly everyone *chose* to be born into this life. They chose their gender, their country, their parents, their period in history and the actual timing of their birth. And nearly all recalled seeing the foetus and merging with it after a sojourn elsewhere, often very shortly before the birth itself was due. Many remarked on how incongruous it seemed to be an entity with an adult mind choosing to be born again as a little baby.

Physical Phenomena

The cases I have described so far have, essentially, been based upon the *perceptions* of particular individuals. However, there are also numerous cases on record in which unexplained *physical* phenomena have been observed and, in many cases, photographed. Crop circles, whatever their origins, are a well-known example of this, as are photographic 'orbs' and Unidentified Flying Objects (UFOs). The next case is an unusual one, but is well authenticated, having been reported in the press at the time:

Case 20: The 'Devil's Hoof Marks'

On the morning of 9th February 1855, during one of England's severest winters of the nineteenth century, there had been a two-inch covering of snow during the night. In South Devon, as in many other places that morning, the snow layer was pristine and unbroken, except for a few animal tracks. But there was something very unusual about one particular track. Starting in a garden on the outskirts of Totnes, the track zigzagged across South Devon, covering a distance of some 100 miles, finishing at Littleham, near Exmouth. At one point, the track even crossed the estuary of the River Exe. The prints themselves were quite unusual, being horseshoe shaped, some four or five inches long and spaced about eight inches apart, in a single file.

Various theories were proposed on what had caused these

mysterious prints, most suggesting that they had been produced by animals, including rats, rabbits and even a kangaroo. However, in different places, whatever had produced the track had scaled a fourteen-foot high wall, passed through a six-inch hole and crawled through a length of drainpipe. (This effectively rules out the kangaroo as a possibility.) The creature, whatever it was, had apparently hopped along on a single cloven hoof, covering an incredibly large distance in one night.

The incident was widely reported in the press but, to this day, no satisfactory explanation has ever been forthcoming. Since it occurred prior to the invention of photography, only hand-drawn sketches of the track exist. Given that the creature had a cloven hoof, and that many people in those days still believed in a horned Devil with cloven feet, the track came to be dubbed the 'Devil's Hoof Marks'.

Crop Circles

The case of the 'Devil's Hoof Marks' is, in a sense, not unlike the better known phenomenon of Crop Circles, as both are cases of physical impressions being left on the ground. Over the last few decades, incidences of Crop Circles have been too numerous for me to identify any as being of special interest. In the simplest cases, a circular area of crops has been flattened into a spiral pattern, although precise measurements have shown that many, if not all, are actually slightly elliptical in shape. It appears that the simplest circles are a natural phenomenon, caused by some kind of atmospheric vortex. Common sense would dismiss the more elaborate patterns as a hoax and, indeed, it has been demonstrated on television that it is not unduly difficult to make them. Notwithstanding this, certain observations are to be made, especially concerning the more elaborate patterns:

- All of the crop formations appear to have been produced within a very short period of time, often overnight.

- There are generally no reports of footprints being left in the vicinity of a crop formation.
- Nearly all crop formations, however large and complex, show a degree of precision and sharp definition that would be difficult for any hoaxer to achieve, especially if they did it at night.
- There are apparently no cases of a hoaxer being caught in the act.
- There are apparently no cases of a crop formation being badly executed or left unfinished.
- Similar formations have sometimes been observed in sand, or in similar landscapes (other than crop fields).

It has to be noted, also, that trespass and damaging the crops in this manner is a criminal offence under British Law, although I know of only one successful prosecution in this instance. I do not know whether the alleged perpetrator was actually caught in the act.

The overall picture that emerges is that, while many crop formations are probably hoaxes, there have been a few which defy explanation.

Case 21: The Bélmez Faces

An especially bizarre incident occurred in the village of Bélmez de la Moraleda in southern Spain, in the summer of 1971. Again, this involved the ground becoming physically marked in some way. A child playing on the kitchen floor noticed the distinct image of a human face in the tiles around the hearth. To the child, this was simply an amusing game, but when the grandmother saw the face, she was terrified, especially as the face bore an agonized expression. The family immediately ripped up the tiles, destroying the face, and laid a new concrete floor. But three weeks later, another face appeared in the concrete, again bearing an agonized expression. By now, the public authorities had heard about the faces, and were becoming involved. They refused to let the family destroy the second image, and ordered the removal of that whole section of floor for scientific study. A chemical analysis identified several different minerals in the concrete, but there was no evidence that the image had been painted onto the concrete, or otherwise tampered with. Other faces continued to appear in the floor and walls of the building.

A research team decided to excavate the kitchen floor and, nine feet down, they found that the house had been built on top of an ancient cemetery. According to one report, ultra-sensitive microphones were installed in the house; these detected faint voices, below the threshold of human hearing, speaking strange languages and making agonized moans.

It is of interest to note that the grandmother, Mariá Gómez, was known locally as a psychic medium.

If the reports of Sylvan Muldoon and Robert Monroe (re 'astral travelling') are to be accepted, along with the case of the Bélmez Faces, then it may be inferred that man has some kind of 'spirit body' which can, under some circumstances, impress an image onto solid matter, even if that matter happens to be inanimate material. The process would be not unlike that of magnetic fields being rendered visible by a sprinkling of iron filings, as many of us will recall from school physics lessons. This brings us to the topic of physical phenomena as observed at séances. Spiritualist meetings have been conducted in various parts of the world for at least a century and a half, and there is much documented evidence. I shall have more to say on this in the next chapter, but first I must report on a particularly interesting experiment that was carried out in Norfolk, England, in the 1990s.

Case 22: The Scole Experiment

This was a series of events, rather than a single event, but since they all took place in the same location and involved the same research team, it is legitimate to treat these as a single case. Details of the experiments are given in the book *The Scole Experiment* by Grant and Jane Solomon.

In early 1993, an already established psychic circle, based at Scole in Norfolk, received an ostensible spirit communication saying that conditions were now right for a special experimental project to begin. The purpose of this was to demonstrate to a scientifically literate public irrefutable proof of human survival after death. The project was conducted and the results assessed by Mr Montague Keen and Professors Arthur Ellison and David Fontana, all of whom were investigators from the Society for Psychical Research (SPR).

At least 37 sessions were conducted in a blacked-out room in which a number of phenomena such as raps, taps, light flashes, levitations and apports (objects appearing 'out of thin air') were regularly observed. On one occasion, Professor Fontana was asked to place his hand in a Pyrex bowl, in which (in the darkness) he felt a crystal. When he was asked to do so again, a few seconds later, the crystal had gone. On the third occasion (again, a few seconds later) the crystal was back in its original position.

Also, on several occasions, photographic colour films were brought into the room, still in their original packaging. These were placed inside a sealed box, which was left intact for the entire session. The films were developed immediately upon removal from their packaging, revealing a series of elaborate glyphs and designs that no camera could have produced. (Solomon's book includes a number of coloured illustrations of these.)

The communicators gave instructions for the construction of a piece of apparatus involving a germanium semiconductor and a tape-recorder without a microphone connected. This would enable them to communicate directly with the sitters. Significant communications were received using this apparatus but sadly, sometime later, the researchers decided to terminate the experiment. They feared that they might be opening up channels to potentially unfriendly alien communicators, and were not prepared to take such a risk.

Case 23: The Student without a Brain

Sometime during the 1970s (I do not have an exact date) the campus doctor at Sheffield University examined a mathematics student who had come in to see him about a minor medical complaint. The student had an IQ of 126 and was expected to graduate. Noting that the student's head was somewhat enlarged, the doctor referred him to Professor John Lorber, suggesting a CAT scan of the student's head to check for hydrocephalus (a collection of fluid on the brain). Amazingly, the scan revealed that the young man had virtually no physical brain at all, only a very thin layer of cerebral tissue at the top of his spinal cord. Despite his physical condition, the student was not only able to live a normal life, but went on to gain an Honours degree in mathematics.

This case suggests that the physical brain is only a part of a much larger system which also includes electric and magnetic fields. This raises the question: if someone can think without a brain, could they also think if the entire physical body were missing? (In which case, the person would be invisible – a 'ghost', in fact.) This would appear to be the case.

(This case was first reported in a science journal in 1980. Further information on this and similar cases may be accessed by googling 'John Lorber'.)

Before concluding this chapter, I think a word needs to be said about some cases of apparent coincidence. Common sense would say that 'coincidence' is just that – coincidence. But when strings of coincidences appear to happen to the same person or group of people, things become more interesting. Are these just 'coincidences', or is something more significant happening? Is the universe trying to tell us something? The following two cases are interesting, but I make no judgement regarding any deeper significance they might have.

Case 24: Abraham Lincoln and John F Kennedy

The parallels between the lives and subsequent assassinations of US Presidents Abraham Lincoln and John F Kennedy are fairly well known and are well documented. The main points here are:

- Lincoln was elected to the House of Representatives in 1846, Kennedy in 1946.
- Lincoln was runner-up for the party's nomination for vice-president in 1856, Kennedy in 1956.
- Lincoln was elected President in 1860, Kennedy in 1960.
- Both presidents sought to address the problems of black Americans.
- Both presidents lost a son during their presidency.
- Both presidents were shot in the head from behind.
- Lincoln was in Ford's Theatre when he was shot; Kennedy was in a car made by the Ford motor company (a Lincoln convertible).
- Lincoln's assassin fled from the theatre to a warehouse; Kennedy's assassin fled from a warehouse to a theatre.
- Both assassins were themselves killed before they could be put on trial.
- Both presidents were succeeded by a president called Johnson.
- Andrew Johnson was born in 1808, Lyndon B Johnson in 1908.

There have been attempts to debunk this information. The historic facts are easy enough to check, however, and this list of apparent coincidences is impressive. I pass no judgement at this point, but I shall give another example of apparent parallel destinies between two famous people:

Case 25: Princess Diana and Marilyn Monroe

There are parallels between the lives of Princess Diana and Marilyn Monroe, which, so far as I am aware, have not been noted or commented upon elsewhere, but which are interesting. The main points here are:

- Princess Diana and Marilyn Monroe were both blonde women who were public icons.
- Both had connections with people in high places: Princess Diana married into the British Royal Family; Marilyn Monroe was a close friend of President John F Kennedy.
- Both had birthdays on the first of the month.
- There have been suspicions surrounding the deaths of both women.
- Both were subject of Elton John's song *Candle in the Wind* (a deliberate choice made by Elton John himself).
- Most tantalizing of all – both lived for *exactly* 13,210 days (36 years and 61 days).

The list is less impressive than that regarding Lincoln and Kennedy, and again I pass no judgement. Ultimately there is no certain way of deciding whether such strings of apparent coincidences are meaningful in any way.

Minor coincidences crop up on a daily basis for virtually everyone and these are, usually quite rightly, dismissed as insignificant. They are often forgotten after a day or two. To give an example from my own life: my parents first met at the Oxford Galleries, a dance-hall in Newcastle upon Tyne; my brother was married at Oxford Street Methodist Church in Whitley Bay and then, a few years later, I moved to Oxford to teach there. It is very probable that, these connections with the name 'Oxford' are no more than coincidental.

In this chapter, I have endeavoured to use case materials that are verifiable from historic and other written accounts. I cannot, of course, *guarantee* that every case recounted here is genuine, but even if only a handful of them are, this is a sufficient indication that something very interesting is going on. We clearly don't know *all* of the laws of physics; if we did, then research physicists would be out of a job. The historical records may or may not be accurate, and hoaxes have long been rife. As a scientist, therefore, I must therefore judge all such recorded cases with an element of scepticism.

All knowledge must, in the first instance, come from direct observation. Accurate observation and repeatable experiments are the gold standard of all scientific work, and the process of peer review ought to ensure at least a common consensus on the nature of the world in which we live. But I have yet add my own experiences, which are at least as interesting, and which are the subject of the next chapter.

2: Even Scientists Dream

The importance of direct observation and accurate recording in scientific work can never be over-emphasized. In the laboratory, this is often a simple business: we take measurements, do the calculations and (sometimes) form a hypothesis. In addition to this, however, we all dream – even scientists. August Kekulé's dream about the benzene molecule, likening it to a snake swallowing its own tail, is a classic example.

Dreamland is a funny place where the laws of physics (and common sense) are temporarily suspended. Geography goes haywire, with familiar places being transformed beyond recognition from how they appear in real life. And yet, in the dream state, we take all of this for granted. But sometimes – on very rare occasions – we happen to notice these anomalies and suddenly become aware that we are dreaming. This is known as *lucid dreaming* and some researchers have linked this with out-of-body experiences.

Even in dreamland, accurate observation of the dream content is often possible, especially if the dream is a vivid one. Dreams are quickly forgotten, however, and so, if one wishes to make a serious study of them, written records are essential – a dream diary. Even if the dream is a vivid one it is generally useful to keep a written record of it for future reference.

Over the years, I have had my own share of interesting and vivid dreams, some of which have turned out to be quite instructive. I begin with a number of the most significant dreams I have had, starting with two from the time when I was about five years old:

The Volcano

At the time of this first dream, I was living in a small bungalow which backed onto a cornfield, on the outskirts of Bishop

Auckland. In the dream, I saw this same field covered in fine white cinder ash to a depth of about a foot. This was similar to the white ash that accumulates beneath a coal fire. In the background was the huge black shape of a volcano with a dull red glow at its summit. Later, when I saw the volcano broadside on, it looked much larger, and the glow on the summit had brightened to a vivid yellow. The sky was dark, and there was an oppressive, suffocating feel in the air. I had a strong impression that this was something I had remembered from a very long time ago – possibly over a period of several millennia.

What is significant about this dream is that, at that age, *no one had ever told me that there were such things as volcanoes.* Yet when I later learnt about volcanoes from books and school geography lessons, it turned out that the details of the dream – the volcanic ash – the dark sky – the oppressive atmosphere – were all factually correct. *So how did I obtain this information?*

The Theatre

In the second dream, I found myself travelling north with a group of people, toward what I took to be the Scottish border. I had the impression that these people were mainly members of my father's side of the family, whom I had known for a long time. On the left-hand side of the road was a red-brick building; it had a glass porch having a faded yellow number six painted on the windows, on either side. Looming ahead in the distance was the ominous black shape of a huge mountain with a flattened summit, where I could discern the burnt-out remains of an old abbey. We skirted the eastern side of the mountain and arrived in the back yard of a rather humble terraced house. All of my companions entered the house, leaving me alone in the yard. After waiting for some time I entered of my own volition and found a group of people standing in a circle in the kitchen. It appeared that they were there to advise me on something. Whilst they were still deliberating, however, I entered a pair of glass doors on the right and found myself inside a theatre. But this was no ordinary theatre! A blank cinema screen at the front emitted a low hum, similar to that of an electrical transformer, And along the aisle, at the ends of the rows of seats, were a series of lamps with glass, flame-shaped 'heads' and brass stands. All of the lamps, except the big one at the back, had faces and seemed to be looking at me, while the large, faceless lamp had bands of colour around the bottom of the globe. There was an eerie feeling about this scene, and I didn't like it. And so I closed my eyes and walked down to a small doorway to the left of the cinema screen, where I exited. Outside, there was a large lake next to a redbrick pumping station. At the edge of the lake was a man singing. It was at this point in the dream that I woke.

The memory of this dream continued to disturb me well into my adulthood until, in 1979, the penny dropped. The BBC's science programme *Tomorrow's World* included a feature on 'womb music'. Evidently, the foetus hears a low hum while it is still in the womb, very similar to the sound that I heard in my dream. The interpretation of my dream suddenly became clear. The 'lamps' were the foetus – *my* foetus – and the big lamp with no face was the placenta. The memory of this dream no longer troubles me, but its implications are profound. Not only did I 'remember' being born, but I recall also entering the womb from outside and joining with the foetus, having already lived another life elsewhere.

On numerous occasions, during my adult life, I have had dreams which were definitely of either a telepathic or precognitive nature. Several of these are of interest here, and are worth recounting:

The Young Lion

In March 1972, I had a vivid dream in which the postman arrived at the house (actually my previous home at the time of the dream) and delivered to us a young lion. It wasn't a cub, but neither it was it fully grown. I noted especially the animal's sleek, brown coat. The postman told us that we had won it as a prize in a competition run by the *Reader's Digest* magazine. We didn't know what to do with this lion, and tied it to a table leg to stop it from running around the house.

The following afternoon, I bought the then current edition of the *Reader's Digest* magazine. Inside was an article about two young men who had adopted a young lion as a pet (naming it Christian), and who later released it into the wild. There were pictures of the lion in the magazine, and it was identical to the one I had seen in my dream.

Tom Tower, Oxford

In December 1981 I had been teaching for some years at a small private college in Oxford, not far from the city's famous Tom Tower, which forms the gateway to Christchurch College. In the dream, I saw the tower and heard the clock strike. I immediately (in the dream) interpreted this as a sign that 'Tom' would be coming to the college. This was followed by a scene in which the college bursar was clearing away all the books from the library shelves. The science books had already gone, and he was now clearing the rest of the shelves.

When I arrived back at the college after the Christmas vacation, at least twenty members of the academic staff, including myself, were given notices of redundancy. The science courses at the college were to be discontinued altogether. The director who issued the redundancy notices was called Tom – and yes, he *did* come to the college to supervise the proceedings.

Yuri Andropov

Yuri Andropov served as Prime Minister of the Soviet Union for a short period during the early 1980s. In 1984, I had a particularly vivid dream in which a group of us were standing in a country roadway which was bordered by a low hedge. Standing in the middle of the field, on the other side of the hedge, was Yuri Andropov. He was in a really angry mood, waving his arms around and shouting at us. But it wasn't clear in the dream what he was angry about. On waking, I saw that the time was nearly seven o'clock, and so I put the radio on to hear the news. The headlines were that Yuri Andropov had died.

The 'Challenger' Shuttle Disaster

In January 1986, I had a slightly bizarre dream in which I saw a double image of a clock face and, at the same time, heard the words, 'She died at the height of her glory' (or words to similar effect). The dream occurred in the early hours of 28th January – the date of the *Challenger* shuttle disaster – the event itself occurring several hours *after* my dream. One of the victims of the disaster was schoolteacher Christa McAuliffe who was the first civilian to be launched into space. This was indeed (or should have been) her 'moment of glory'.

The only puzzle in this dream was the image of the clock faces – apparently a double image. Perhaps this was meant as a visual indicator that I was looking ahead in time.

The Piper Alpha Disaster

In 1988, I had a rather gloomy dream in which I was looking across what I took to be the North Sea. A waning moon in the sky looked ominously like a malevolent eye staring across the scene. This dream occurred almost simultaneously with the Piper Alpha disaster, which, of course, was located in the North Sea.

Miinnehoma

In 1994, on the morning of England's *Grand National* horse race, I dreamt that I was looking at a map of North America in which the US State of Minnesota was highlighted. At the time of the dream, I did not know what horses would be running that day, but I do normally place a bet on the Grand National. When I looked through the list of horses that were running that day, the name *Miinnehoma* immediately caught my attention, and reminded me of my dream. It was a strange feeling as I walked up to the betting office: I *knew* that this horse was going to win. It earned me the princely sum of £44.

Of course, I cannot *prove* to anyone else what dreams I have had in the past (or indeed at any time), and so none of these dreams can be of any evidential value to other people – especially the scientific community. I can, nevertheless, assure the reader that all of the dreams recounted above are genuine ones from my own experience. They are of evidential value to myself, if to no one else.

Have I Lived Before?

The first two dreams I recounted earlier in this chapter seemed to imply that I had lived some kind of life prior to my present one here on earth. The picture is much bigger than this, however. From other childhood dreams and impressions, which I still recall, I have an impression of having lived on this earth at least *fourteen* times. It seems that I started my incarnation cycle in central/southern Africa and then migrated around the world in a westerly direction. I have fragmentary impressions of an ancient civilization which used electric lamps and air ionizers, and that I was fatally burnt in an accident involving a lamp. I also have an impression of flying over the Pacific Ocean and seeing it punctuated by a series of long, finger-like islands and peninsulas (which no longer exist); and I have later impressions of past lives in China, India, Greece, Spain, France, Bohemia and Austria.

My impressions of Bohemia and Austria are the most vivid, as they refer to what I feel was my most recent sojourn here on earth. It seems that I was born in southern Bohemia in the early 1840s, grew up in Vimperk (which I have identified from pictures of the town) and later moved to the Vorarlberg area of Austria, where I worked as a clockmaker. I liked this work very much but, in 1895 or 1896, I was caught in an avalanche whilst out walking. I had the impression of ascending into the sky and looking down at the mountainside where the avalanche had just claimed me. I was 52 or 53 years of age at the time, and felt disappointed that I would no longer be able to continue in clockmaking, a job which I had loved so much.

Are these impressions genuine, or are they mere figments of my own imagination? It is impossible to tell. It *may* be possible to check out some of the details of this last 'incarnation' against any documentary evidence that might still exist – but this could be a long shot. However, given the success that Helen Wambach had with her subjects, this possibility cannot be ruled out.

Remote Viewing

In recent years I have sat in a meditation circle at Jenny's Sanctuary, a small spiritualist centre located near Banbury, Oxfordshire. On numerous occasions, whilst in meditation, I have received visual impressions of houses and gardens belonging to other sitters, and have given accurate descriptions of many of the scenes. On at least two occasions I have received sufficient feedback to know that the impressions were veridical. On one occasion I saw a through lounge in someone's house with large mirrors above the fireplaces, on the right. I later visited that house and found that my impressions were largely (though not completely) accurate. In another meditation I saw an unusual candlestick in the style of a Roman caduceus. The lady who owned this item later brought it in and showed it to me.

The overall impression I have gained from all of these experiences is that 'consciousness' – whatever it may be – is something which transcends not only the physical brain and sense organs, but even the limits of time and space.

The next section is devoted to a type of experience that is so subjective that, to my knowledge, no one has ever previously written about it. Indeed, the scientific community has yet to acknowledge that the phenomenon even exists. It relates to how we perceive space and form mental maps of our environment. I believe that this is part of everyone's perception of the landscape – but the effect is so subtle that hardly anyone seems to notice it. I think I must be unique in having made any kind of systematic study of it.

The Hidden Compass

Imagine the following scenario. You have just arrived in a town that you have never visited before. You walk up the main street which, let us say, leads north. You turn to the left (west) and continue along that street – but you fail to notice that the street bends slightly to the left. Further on, you again turn left (thinking now that you are going south), and fail to notice that that street also bends to the left. You turn left once more and – quite unexpectedly – you find yourself back in the main street where you started. But the main street now looks *different*. The buildings and lighting are exactly the same as before, but

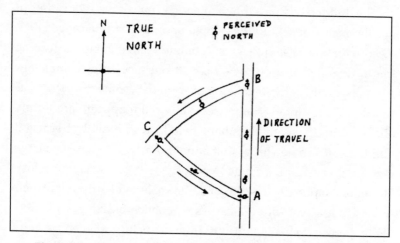

Fig. 1: The 'Inner Compass': how people become disoriented

'something' has changed. The sensation of seeing the main street transformed in this manner is often unsettling and can leave many people feeling confused and bewildered. This is what 'disorientation' is really all about, and it explains why many people have a poor 'sense of direction'. So what exactly has happened?

Common sense says that the street itself could not have changed. It is your perception of which way is 'north' that has changed, not the street. The fact is that your 'inner compass' has, imperceptibly, rotated anticlockwise through an angle of ninety degrees – so that what you now think is north is really west. And so it looks as if the street has rotated ninety degrees clockwise.

Your 'inner compass' may actually take any of four basic orientations with respect to the street, which is thus seen in one of four different 'aspects'. This phenomenon is fundamental to all of our perception of space, but we usually fail to notice it. For my own part, I find it quite impossible to imagine any region in space – even 'empty' space – without also visualizing my 'inner compass' pointing in some direction or other. I cannot even conceive what any actual landscape or townscape must be 'really' like, once the 'inner compass' effect is removed.

The 'hidden compass' phenomenon is one of the root causes (if not the main cause) of why people become lost in strange cities. 'Disorientation' is simply a result of one's 'inner compass' turning this way and that, until one has lost one's bearings completely. Animals, on the other hand, do not seem to become disoriented as we do. Their 'inner compasses', it would appear, are firmly aligned with the earth's magnetic field instead of with streets and buildings. It is noteworthy that animals are able to navigate large distances, even in strange territory, without becoming lost. Humans cannot do this. Because animals evidently align their 'inner compasses' with the earth's magnetic field, they will, most likely, perceive streets and buildings as being oriented at skew angles. This would be highly disconcerting for us humans, but it would seem that for animals it is normal.

The 'hidden compass' phenomenon strongly suggests that there is no such thing as seeing the world as it 'really' is. Everyone's view of the world is subjective – and different. And every person's view of the world is just as valid as any other.

Dowsing

In recent years I have learnt the art of dowsing. The popular image of dowsing is that of a person using a forked twig of witch-hazel to locate underground sources of water – a technique which has been demonstrated to work. I have not used this method, but I have done other forms of dowsing using either a quartz pendulum or a pair of angle-rods.

The angle-rods are pieces of stout wire bent into an 'L' shape, some 10 to 15 inches long, and are held, one in each hand, with the stem (the longer part) of the 'L' pointing straight forward. Using this technique, it is possible to detect underground water sources (as with the witch-hazel twig), also ley lines (magnetic anomalies in the earth's surface) and the outer boundary of a person's aura – a kind of electromagnetic field that surrounds every living person. When the rods respond, they swivel through ninety degrees so that they are pointing in toward each other. However, for some individuals (usually women) the rods may turn to point outward instead of inward – this is not significant. I have successfully used the rods to detect ley lines and people's auric fields. Incredibly, I have also used the rods to locate a mislaid plastic soap-dish, to tell the time and to ascertain the best route for driving from Banbury to Newcastle – by dowsing a road atlas!

The pendulum is a weight (not necessarily of quartz, although this is what I normally use) suspended from a light chain or length of cord, some six to ten inches long. The top end of the chain or cord is held between the user's thumb and forefinger. The user starts by establishing a 'yes-no' response from the pendulum by asking it questions which have an obvious answer (e.g. 'Is my name Fred?'). The pendulum will respond by swinging or gyrating in a certain pattern: clockwise for a 'yes' and anticlockwise for a 'no' is a typical response. It is advisable to do this at the beginning of every session, as the pendulum's responses may change over time and can also vary from person to person. While none of my own experiences with the pendulum is of special interest here, I was greatly impressed when my brother (an architect – and an arch-sceptic) told me that a colleague had successfully used a dowsing pendulum and a map to locate a water-main leak at an industrial site in Gateshead, Tyne and Wear. The colleague was sitting in an office in *Sussex* when he performed this exercise.

The Rollright Stones, in North Oxfordshire, are a good place to practise dowsing. One doesn't even have to 'believe' in dowsing to get a result. But leave your magnetic compass at home! A friend took one there once and it became demagnetized. She had to buy a new one.

Spirit Séances

I have saved the best until last. I could easily have recounted other people's experiences of séances but, having been to some myself, I have decided that first-hand experience is the best. And, unlike the dreams and subjective impressions which I recounted earlier, I have plenty of friends who have witnessed the same events that I have done.

Cases of allegedly fraudulent mediumship have, in the past, been rife and so the precautions that have to be taken against possible fraud are necessarily very strict. The medium is securely tied into a chair and gagged, so that any spoken communications cannot possibly be coming from him or her. The chair itself is located in a curtained 'cabinet' at one end of the room. The sitters (people attending the séance) are not allowed to take any loose objects into the room: pockets have to be emptied and shoes, watches, jewellery, money and mobile phones (switched off) all have to be left outside. The medium and sitters are all searched as they enter the room, to ensure that this requirement is met. (This is not unlike airport security.) Once the session is ready to start, the door is sealed and the room is blacked out. A prayer for protection is said, and then loud music is played while the medium goes into a trance. After a few minutes, a spirit communicator will normally 'come through' and greet the sitters. Other communicators may follow later. Usually there are spectacular displays involving flying 'trumpets' – open-ended cones of cardboard or thin sheet metal, with luminous stickers attached. The trumpets often whizz and gyrate through the air at incredible speeds. Often the sitters are asked all to join hands as proof that no (physical) person present in the room is doing any of this. Sometimes the 'deceased' friends and relatives of persons in the room will come through and speak to them. The recipients of such messages are nearly always grateful to hear once more from their loved ones who have 'passed over'. I have been 'visited' in this manner by my father (who passed over in 1992) and from a close friend, also deceased, who threw me a chocolate bar across the room (good shot in the dark!). I have also experienced at first hand the dematerialization of a physical object. Some spirit communicators (children) dismantled a set of bongo drums and threw the pieces around the room. One of the bolts landed behind my back and ended up wedged against the back of chair. Later, when the children announced that they were about to reassemble the drums, the bolt that was wedged behind my back was instantly dematerialized. I felt it go.

(As a postscript to this last section, I had already typed it up previously, duly clicking on 'save' after every paragraph. At the end of the afternoon, however, I suddenly found that none of this work had actually been saved. Most annoying! Perhaps someone 'out there' was trying to tell me something.)

3: Does Astrology Work?

'Astrology' is a taboo word among scientists. This is largely understandable since, at first sight, there is no credible mechanism whereby the positions and alignments of the planets might have any effect on events taking place here on the earth. Because of the distances involved, the gravitational effects of bodies other than the sun or moon are much too weak to have any observable effects on our own environment. Also, any 'astrology' based on the positioning of planets within the constellations can have no physical validity, since the constellations themselves are merely arbitrary patterns delineated in the stellar background.

Let us first be clear on what 'astrology' really is: it is the study of *possible* correlations between the planetary positions and alignments, and events taking place here on the earth. Such correlations (if observed) may, of course, be subjective, and no presumptions are made about a possible causal link if such correlations do indeed turn out to be genuine.

As always, accurate observation is of paramount importance, and this applies as much in astrology as in any other field of study. Because of the complexity of the subject, systematic studies are difficult to arrange, but a few such studies have been carried out, notably by Hans Eysenck and Michel Gauquelin. It is essential that any researchers conducting such studies do so with an open mind. And if, by any chance, a body of evidence emerges which suggests that astrology *might* work, at least in principle, then this needs to be taken seriously.

Is there already a body of evidence suggesting that astrology might work? Nearly all scientists would say 'no'. But things are not as clear-cut as this. Hans Eysenck did a study in which he assessed a number of subjects on the extroversion-introversion scale and correlated the results according to the astrological signs under which those subjects were born. His finding was that people born under the odd-numbered signs (Aries, Gemini, Leo, Libra, Sagittarius and Aquarius) were significantly more extroverted than those born under any of the other six signs, with Taurus and Virgo being particularly strongly introverted.

Traditional astrology is a vast and complex subject, however, and has little to do with people being 'born under' this or that astrological sign. It takes into account also the positions of the moon and planets in the sky, the angles ('aspects') they make to one another as seen from the earth, and whether any of them is close to either the horizon or the north-south meridian.

The other major study with which many may be familiar was conducted by the Belgian investigator, Michel Gauquelin. In his survey, he studied the astrological charts of a number of professional people who were successful in their own fields, noting whether there were any common factors that linked the charts for members of a particular profession. He found that for the most successful athletes, the planet Mars had just recently passed either the horizon (east or west) or the meridian (north or south), dubbing this observation 'the Mars effect'. He also found that for doctors and scientists, Saturn tended to occupy a similar position. For actors it was Jupiter, and for writers it was the Moon. For politicians, either Jupiter or the Moon (or both) showed a tendency to occupy this position. Overall, these findings are significant, but also interesting in that they appear to *contradict* traditional astrology – which has always stated that planets are 'weakened' when placed in these areas of the astrological chart.

An interesting, but little-known, study by the US astrologer, Edward O Hammack Jr suggests that, as the planet Saturn progresses along its orbit, over a 29½-year period, successively making different angles to the position of the Sun in our birth charts, we experience alternating 'positive' (favourable) and 'negative' (less favourable) periods of approximately seven years each, changing polarity whenever the angle between transiting Saturn and our natal position of the Sun reaches a multiple of ninety degrees. We thus experience a double cycle as Saturn completes its orbit.

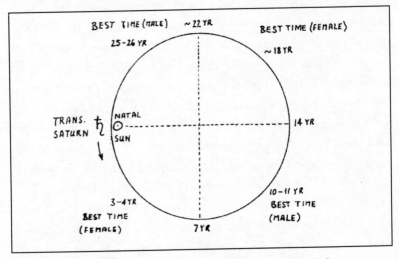

Fig. 2: Hammack's Astrology: the Basic Principle

Strangely, he suggests that the 'positive' periods for a man are 'negative' for a woman with the same birthday, and vice versa. (The case of transgender people is a moot point here.) I have tested this theory on a number of my friends and relatives and, while I have noted a few exceptions, Hammack's system does *in principle* appear to work.

To give a few case studies, in 1932, when Sir Winston Churchill was at one of his 'worst' times (according to Hammack) his warnings about German militarism were being ignored. When he became UK Prime Minister he was at his 'best' time, but he went on to lose the 1945 General Election at his next 'worst' time. At his next 'best' time he had become Prime Minister again, and also won the Nobel Prize for Literature.

Like Churchill, Adolf Hitler lost an election at one of his

'worst' times, in 1928. In 1933, having just entered the 'positive' half of the cycle, he became German Chancellor until, by 1936, he was at the height of his power – and full of belligerence. By 1939 was feeling confident enough to start a war. His 'worst' time came again in 1943 when his health was deteriorating, and he had just lost the Battle of Stalingrad. He committed suicide two years later.

Margaret Thatcher was experiencing a 'best' time when Prime Minister Edward Heath appointed her as Minister of Education in the early 1970s. At the end of the 'positive' phase her party lost the General Election (in October 1974), but (paradoxically) she was elected party leader in 1975. She had just reached the end of her 'worst' time (in 1978) when her party won the 1979 General Election and she became Prime Minister. Once in office, however, she and her party soon lost popularity, only to regain it after the Falklands War in 1982. At this point, Margaret had just re-entered the 'positive' phase of the cycle. At her next 'best' time, in 1986, she was working with Presidents Reagan and Gorbachev to bring about an end to the Cold War. By 1990, however, she had once more entered the 'negative' phase of the cycle and had lost popularity again. She resigned as Prime Minister and party leader in November of that year.

(Sadly, Hammack's excellent book *Complete Book of Practical Astrology* has, at the time of writing, long been out of print, but second-hand copies should still be obtainable.)

Traditional astrology teaches that planets positioned at intervals of 180, 90 or 45 degrees, as seen from the earth, exert a 'stressful' influence, which is transitory as far as external events are concerned, but which can have a lasting effect upon people who were born during such periods. Astrologers call these 'difficult' aspects. Planets positioned at intervals of 120 or 60 degrees, conversely, are deemed to have a more relaxing effect, and are dubbed 'easy' aspects. There is universal agreement among astrologers on this.

On the face of it, there does appear to be some validity in this: I have noted time and again that people born during periods when the planets were predominantly spaced at 90-degree intervals tend to be tense, driven and generally quite stubborn, whereas those born when the planets were spaced predominantly at 60- or 120-degree intervals are generally more laid-back. Studies of the 11-year sunspot cycle suggest that there may be an actual physical basis for this. In the 1940s, John Nelson, a young radio engineer, was hired by RCA to investigate how short-wave radio communications might be improved. He found that this was significantly influenced by the sunspot cycle, and also that sunspot maxima tended to occur when the planets Jupiter and Saturn were (roughly) in a straight line with the sun. It is at these times that the sun's magnetic field reverses its direction. The positions of Uranus and Neptune (the other 'heavy' planets), which are farther out and slower moving than Jupiter and Saturn, have been observed to have a weaker and longer term effect upon the incidence of sunspots.

The observation of natural physical events ought (in theory) to provide some of the best evidence of whether astrology works. Earthquakes make an especially good study in this respect since, with modern technology, their timing and geographic location can be precisely determined. And – most importantly – there is no possibility of any human intervention in their incidence.

Anyone with astrological software can draw up the astro-logical charts of the major earthquakes that have occurred over the last century or so, and note the planetary positions. It is beyond the scope of this book to conduct such a survey and report on it, but I have singled out one major earthquake as being of special interest. The great earthquake that struck the city of San Francisco on 18th April 1906 registered 7.9 on the Richter scale and resulted in a 22-foot linear displacement along the San Andreas Fault. At the moment the earthquake struck, the planet

Uranus had *just* passed the southern meridian (known as the 'midheaven' in astrology), while the planet Neptune opposing it, had simultaneously passed the 'nadir' or northern end of the meridian line. At the time, the planet Mercury, in the east, was also making 90-degree angles to both of these planets. Looking at this alignment, it is difficult to escape the conclusion that the major planets Uranus and Neptune must have somehow triggered the earthquake as they simultaneously crossed the opposite ends of the meridian – spurred on, possibly, by Mercury squaring both planets.

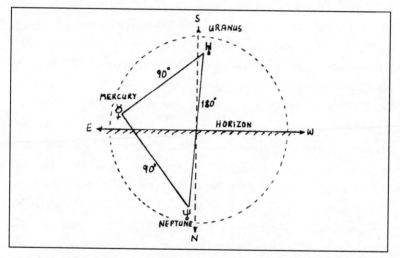

Fig. 3: Planetary Alignment for San Francisco Earthquake, April 1906

A somewhat different approach to astrology was pioneered in the late 1980s by Alan Krakower, a Canadian man who, in later life, adopted the pseudonym of *Ra Uru Hu*. The tale of how he became inspired to produce his system is so extraordinary that it is worth recounting here.

Following a series of professional failures, Krakower had taken a flight to Europe and then a bus to Spain, where, for some unknown reason, a fellow passenger persuaded him to go to the island of Ibiza. On 4th January 1987, while returning to his residence on the island, he saw a glow coming from inside the house. This puzzled him, as there was no electric lighting in the house, and his lamp had run out of oil. Once inside the house, he felt what seemed like an explosion inside his head; then he heard a male voice telling him that it was time to get down to work. For eight days and nights Krakower meticulously transcribed the messages that were allegedly being dictated to him by this mysterious voice. The work that finally evolved from this was the system we now know as *Human Design*.

This system differs radically from traditional astrology in that it divides the zodiac not into twelve 'signs' but into 64 'gates', each of which equates with one of the hexagrams of the *I Ching*. Strangely, the positioning of the gates bears no logical relationship to the positions of either the equinoxes or the fixed stars. The gates (and hexagrams) all have counterparts in one of nine centres within human body (hence the name *Human Design*), each of which is associated with a specific organ of the body. The gates are also linked in pairs, which form 'channels' between the centres.

Under Krakower's system, an astrological chart is drawn up for the date and time of the person's birth, and also for the time three months previously when the sun was at a *precise* angle of 88 degrees from its birth position. The planetary positions for both dates are located in the appropriate gates on the astrological map. This information is then transferred to a 'bodygraph' in which the gates with occupying planets (said to be 'defined') are marked. Where the gates at both ends of a channel are thus defined, the channel itself is likewise said to be defined, as are the centres containing those gates. Software is available which will perform the calculations and produce the bodygraph.

The system as a whole is complex and seemingly arbitrary. It ignores such factors as the zodiac signs, the 'house' positions of the planets and the aspects (angles) between different planets, all of which are fundamental in traditional astrology. However, as for any astrologically based system, the proof of the pudding has to be in the eating, and I am aware that there are a number of serious-minded people (many of them professionals) who accept *Human Design* as a valid system and use it in their work.

Looking at the *Human Design* system with an astronomer's eye, I do consider it to be flawed, despite plausible claims that it actually works. The reason for my scepticism is that there is apparently no sensible provision for taking into account the precession of the equinoxes. Are the 'gates', into which the zodiac is supposedly divided, rooted into the stellar background – or do they follow the earth's precession? The latter seems highly improbable, as there is no neat correspondence between the gates and the tropical zodiac signs, but there is also no obvious reference point among the fixed stars.

Out of interest, I have drawn up my own *Human Design* chart, both by the 'official' method and also by applying what I consider an appropriate correction for precession. My overall impression is that the chart corrected for precession gives a truer picture than the 'official' one, although my judgement on this is probably subjective.

In my mind, the jury is still out on whether *Human Design* is a valid system. But it is, to say the least, interesting.

On the face of it, there does appear to be sufficient empirical evidence that astrology *could* work, at least in principle, although the effect must necessarily be a subtle one. If it doesn't work then, of course, the story ends there and we may as well burn our astrology books. However, as we shall see later, it is conceivable that some of theories of modern physics, when combined, have ramifications that may account for at least *some* of the phenomena we call 'astrology'. Possibilities for such a working physical model will be discussed later in this book. However, I will say at this point that if space is smooth and continuous (as it appears to be on the macro scale), then it is difficult to see how astrology could 'work' in any physical sense. But if space is pixellated ('grainy') – and there is growing evidence that this is probably the case – then we do have the beginnings of a possible scientific explanation of the phenomena which we refer to as 'astrology'.

On a final note, one of the more bizarre concepts in traditional astrology is that of a 'void of course' moon. This is when the moon is nearing the end of the zodiac sign that it is in and is to make no more significant angles to other planets before it leaves that sign. This happens every two and a half days or so, and such periods can vary from a few minutes to more than a day. According to traditional astrology, these are crazy periods when things tend to go haywire and even mechanical systems can seemingly to have a mind of their own. Utter nonsense, most of us would say. However, in 1993, the UK's *Grand National* horse race was held during one of these periods. The starting mechanism failed three times, and only half of the horses ran. The race was duly (excuse the pun) declared 'void'. Maybe there could be something in it after all!

The overall picture that emerges is that astrology *may* work – at least in principle – provided that there is an underlying physical mechanism. This does not, of course, guarantee that everything we might find in astrology textbooks is necessarily correct; nor does it imply that we can predict future events (other than astro-nomical ones) using these methods. Furthermore, it does not exclude the possibility that other 'astrological' factors may be at work which are not found in any textbooks on the subject, and of which we currently have no knowledge. In this book we are looking principally to see whether there might be some *physical* principle which might give the study of astrology some credi-bility. If no such physical principle can be found, then the conclusion must be that astrology is fallacious. Given the evidence we have seen, however, it will, perhaps, be a little surprising if some underlying physical principle cannot be found.

4: The Scientists Investigate

The foregoing chapters have suggested that *something* extraordinary is going on that is not accounted for by the laws of physics as we currently know them. However, anecdotal material such as we have seen so far, no matter how spectacular and seemingly convincing to those who have witnessed such events, does not constitute proof in any scientific sense. Science demands that experiments be set up which can be repeated at will, and which yield predictable results whenever carried out. Repeatable experiments are the gold standard of scientific research. But can the bizarre world of unexplained phenomena be investigated using the tried and tested methods of good scientific research?

Sir Isaac Newton is known to have studied (and indeed practised) both astrology and alchemy but – to the best of our knowledge – he would not have subjected these studies to the type of rigorous investigation that a modern scientific approach would demand. It is unlikely that he would have known of such phenomena as precognition, remote viewing or out-of-body experiences, which we have already discussed. Indeed, it was not until at least the mid nineteenth century that any serious scientific studies were carried out in these areas.

According to the parapsychologist Dean Radin, the scientific view of unexplained phenomena typically goes through four stages:

1) Reports of the phenomena are rejected outright by scientists.
2) Scientists acknowledge that there may be 'something in it', but dismiss the reports as trivial and uninteresting.
3) Scientists suddenly see the reports as potentially very important.

4) The phenomena described in the reports are finally accepted as mainstream science.

Over the years, the vast majority of scientists have been extremely sceptical about unexplained events (especially where the paranormal appears to be implicated), if not downright hostile. This is still the prevalent attitude among scientists today, Richard Dawkins and James Randi being noteworthy opponents of any idea that paranormal phenomena might in any way be genuine. However, there has always been a minority of scientists who have taken the view that there may be something in it, and that this merits a proper scientific investigation.

Two of the early pioneers, both of them eminent scientists in their day, were Sir William Crookes and Sir Oliver Lodge. Both men attended spirit séances, conducted under the strictest of conditions, and were convinced by what they saw. They witnessed at first hand the emanation of 'ectoplasm' from a person sitting as a medium, and saw how deceased people could apparently make themselves visible using this substance – even speaking to the sitters through the agency of this substance. The two scientists also witnessed levitation (including that of people) and the mysterious appearance and disappearance of physical objects.

In 1882, along with fellow investigators Edmund Gurney, Frederic Myers and others, they set up the Society for Psychical Research (SPR), a body dedicated to the strict scientific investigation of unexplained phenomena. The Society continues its work today. Notwithstanding the stringency of its procedures, the Society has, over the years, amassed a substantial body of statistical evidence which strongly suggests that many of the phenomena *are* genuine, and that many of us (if not all) have the powers to perceive and, in some cases, even influence things and events that are located 'elsewhere' both in time and in space.

The types of phenomena investigated by the SPR include:

- Telepathy – the ability to 'read' another person's mind.
- Remote viewing – seeing places or things that are located outside of one's line of sight.
- Precognition – perceiving events that have not yet happened, and which later turn out to be veridical.
- Psychokinesis – the ability to move objects without touching them.
- 'Haunting' – visual, auditory and/or mechanical disturbances occurring (usually repeatedly) at particular locations, without any apparent cause.

One of the early investigators was Professor J B Rhine. He tested people for possible telepathic powers using a special pack of cards known as Zener cards (named after their inventor), comprising twenty-five cards of five different designs (five of each design). The designs used are a cross, a square, a circle, a pair of wavy lines and a 'star' (actually a pentagram).

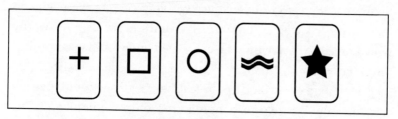

Fig. 4: Zener Cards

In the telepathy experiment, one of the sitters acts as 'transmitter' while the other acts as 'receiver'. The two sitters sit in separate rooms to exclude any possible physical communication between them, but both are able to receive promptings from the experimenter on when to draw or guess a card, and on when the experiment begins or ends. The promptings need not be verbal: a buzzer or bell, which both sitters can hear, is sufficient for this purpose. The 'transmitter' shuffles the pack of cards and draws one at random at regular intervals (as prompted by the experimenter) until the pack is exhausted. The 'receiver', meanwhile, tries to guess the card drawn at each prompt.

In theory, the receiver 'ought' to be able to guess the card correctly for one fifth of the time. This is chance expectation. If the receiver scores more 'hits' than this, then a statistical formula is applied to determine the odds of that result being due to chance alone. The most convincing evidence for telepathy, using this method, has been obtained when the same receiver has consistently obtained above-chance results over a number of trials. There are now, in fact, enough instances on record to indicate that some people do indeed have an apparent ability to perceive correctly what another person is actually experiencing.

On some occasions, during the conduct of this experiment, the receiver has correctly guessed a sequence of cards *before* they were drawn – evidence of *precognition*.

The early experiments using cards did, despite their successes, have certain drawbacks. The receiver would almost certainly know that there were five copies of every card in the pack and that each card would come up five times every 25 guesses (by which time the pack would be exhausted and would need reshuffling). For example, if, after 23 guesses, the receiver realized that the square had only come up three times, he or she could give the square as the last two responses to make up the numbers. This could, at least in theory, skew the outcome of any trial. A good way around this difficulty would therefore be for the transmitter to shuffle the pack *every* time a card is to be drawn, and not just when the pack has been exhausted.

An alternative approach, adopted by later researchers (including Gurney and Myers), has been to use a different type of remote viewing test in which the subject is asked to describe a picture contained in a sealed envelope or, more commonly, to make a drawing of what they 'see'. The subject's description or drawing is then compared with the original. In many such cases, the results have been striking, but there is no obvious 'scientific' method of judging the accuracy of the subject's response.

A way around this latter difficulty has been to for the experimenter to provide a series of different pictures, again all in sealed envelopes, and to select one at random – a blind selection. The remaining pictures then serve as decoys. The subject's drawing is then compared to see which of the sealed pictures it most closely resembles. The evaluation method used here is called *rank-order judging* and entails comparing the remote viewer's responses (whether a drawing or a description) with both the target picture and the decoys. In this case, a positive result is declared if the target picture is ranked as number one more frequently than chance expectation would predict.

Again, in some cases, positive results have been obtained on pictures that were successfully viewed by the subject *before* they had been randomly selected (again a blind selection) – indicating once again that a factor of precognition was also at work. This latter phenomenon has become known as *precognition remote perception* (PRP).

In one interesting case, in which the experimenters varied the procedure by visiting a location selected at random (instead of using pictures) without the subject's knowledge. On one occasion, forty-five minutes *before* a selection had even been made, the subject reported the following:

Rather strange but persistent image of ... a large bowl a hemispheric indentation in the ground of some smooth man-made materials like concrete or cement ...

The site later chosen by the experimenters (not knowing that the subject had already responded) turned out to be the radio telescope at Kitt Peak, Arizona. A 'large bowl' is a good description of such an installation.

By the early 1970s the US government had become interested in the possibility of using remote viewing as a means of gathering military intelligence, and a research project was set up at the Stanford Research Institute (SRI). At the time, this was a think-tank affiliated to Stanford University, but in the late 1970s it became an independent corporation, adopting the name of SRI International – the name it still uses today. The research was conducted by Harold Puthoff and physicist Russell Targ (mentioned in Chapter 1), later to be joined by Edwin May. In their experiments, they would typically give a remote viewer a set of geographic co-ordinates and ask him (it usually was a 'he') to report on what he 'saw' there.

Other experimenters have tried to determine whether it might be possible for a subject to influence the outcome of physical events such as the throwing of dice. Theoretically, each number on a die should have an equal chance of coming up so that a throw of six dice (or six throws of a single die) ought, on average, to yield a total score of 21. The subject is asked to see whether they can 'will' the dice to exceed this total repeatedly when thrown. Again, there is evidence that some people are able to do this.

Further experiments have been carried out in which the subject is tested for possible ESP while placed in a condition of near sensory deprivation. The person wears a 'blindfold' consisting of translucent hemispheres (often made from ping-pong balls cut into two) placed over the eyes, while listening to white noise through headphones. This type of experiment is known as a *ganzfeld* experiment, and was first introduced in the 1970s by Charles Honorton, William Braud and Adrian Parker. (The term *ganzfeld* is a German word meaning 'whole field'.) The objective here is to induce a 'psi conducive' state by reducing the subject's sensory input, since it has long been noted in the past that meditators (who voluntarily reduce their own sensory input) often undergo religious or mystical experiences in which ESP is a factor. The procedure is a seemingly wasteful one in that it takes a team of two or three people some ninety minutes of effort to obtain just a single data point. However, bearing in mind the positive results that have emerged using this method, it has definitely been worth the effort.

Statistical Treatment of Results

It can be argued, quite legitimately, that no single experiment, or even a small number of experiments, however impressive in terms of any positive results it might produce, can necessarily provide conclusive 'proof' that paranormal powers such as ESP actually exist. Good science depends on the collection and statistical processing of large quantities of data. If we take a series of trials using Zener cards as an example, the expected 'hit' rate is normally 20 percent. However, it is common for individual trials to produce results which are significantly higher or lower than this figure.

The standard method of processing the data is first to calculate an average value (known as the *mean*) for all the data points thus obtained, and then apply a formula to calculate a second variable called the *standard deviation*, usually represented by the Greek letter σ (sigma), which indicates how widely the data points are spread around the mean. When plotted graphically, the results show a bell-shaped curve known as the *Gaussian Distribution curve* (Fig. 5). This curve is also sometimes known as the 'normal' distribution curve.

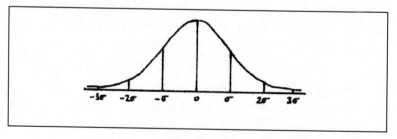

Fig. 5: The Gaussian Distribution Curve

The Gaussian distribution has a remarkable property in that the standard deviation *always* spans the same proportion of data points as shown on the graph. Sixty-eight percent of the data points always lie within one standard deviation of the mean (represented by '0' in the diagram although, in practice, the mean may have any value). Ninety-five percent of the data points are within two standard deviations of the mean, and ninety-nine percent of the data points are within three standard deviations.

What is perhaps more important in this work is the chance that a given data point may lie *outside* the range specified by the standard deviation. The odds against this increase dramatically as the number of standard deviations increases. Thus, the chances of a given data point being outside one standard deviation are about one in three, for two standard deviations ('two sigma') it is about 1 in 22, for three sigma it is about 1 in 370, for four sigma it is about 1 in 15,800 and for five sigma it is about 1 in 1.7 million. (Source: Wikipedia)

Physicists generally use the five-sigma confidence level in their work whereas parapsychologists seem content to use the three-sigma confidence level. (I personally think parapsychologists ought to use the five-sigma confidence level, as physicists do.)

The results from a single experiment, or even a small run of experiments, are generally not sufficient to provide the standard of 'proof' that scientists are looking for. This is generally because the odds against the results being due to chance expectation may not be sufficiently high for any definite conclusion to be drawn. And, of course, experimental procedures must, as always, be *repeatable*. Nevertheless, over the years, many such experiments have been carried out all over the world.

A technique which parapsychologists now use is to harvest the results from *all* published reports of a similar nature and to aggregate them, treating the final result (i.e. the mean) obtained from each *experiment* as a single data point. A new Gaussian distribution is drawn up, giving the mean and standard deviation for all of the means obtained from published sources. This method is known as *meta-analysis*.

Some may argue that *all* of the data points from *every* experiment ought to be aggregated in this manner. There is no real need to do this, however. If most of the results are positive ones then, most likely, the mean for all of these results will also be positive. What is really significant is that most of the reports published so far (spanning several decades) have shown means that were significantly above chance expectation.

There is one further very important point to consider here: not all reports on ESP experiments get published. For all we know, there could be vast numbers of unpublished reports filed away somewhere which contradict any evidence that ESP might exist, and which, if published, could nullify the picture (favouring ESP) already found in the published reports. This is known as the *file-drawer problem*.

ESP researchers and statisticians are fully aware of the file-drawer problem, and have a method of dealing with it. They are able to apply a formula which enables them to calculate how many unpublished 'negative' reports it would take to nullify the positive bias shown in the already published reports. They have already done these calculations and found that, in many cases, the number of 'negative' reports needed to nullify the overall 'positive' picture would have to be absurdly high. In many instances they have found that there would have to be *hundreds of thousands* of unpublished reports for every published one in order to nullify the published results. (A fuller account of the methods of meta-analysis and the file-drawer problem can be found in Dean Radin's book *The Noetic Universe*.)

Work continues in this area, but the overall picture that has emerged from the published reports so far is that extrasensory powers are a real phenomenon, albeit a subtle one. Most of the evidence acquired by experimental investigation has been mundane and seemingly boring in terms of the content of transmitted messages. But then, most good scientific research is based upon the painstaking examination of things that appear mundane, trivial and boring.

When the published experimental evidence is considered together with the anecdotal material from the previous chapters, it becomes evident that there *is* something extraordinary going on, which the known laws of physics and biology cannot explain. It is no longer a question of *whether* such phenomena are genuine; it is a question of what is really going on. The big question facing us now is *how does it all work?* The sciences of physics (the study of the physical world), chemistry (the study of substances) and biology (the study of life processes) have been our main avenues of research so far. But none of these sciences has thus far been able to provide a satisfactory explanation for the kinds of phenomena we have been discussing here. There is clearly still a major gap in our understanding of the nature of things.

In the next section of this book we shall examine our current knowledge of the physical and biological sciences, looking at some of the most recent research, to see whether and to what extent we might be able to provide an explanation of the bizarre phenomena we have been discussing.

II : The Physics

5: What is Time?

Many of the unexplained phenomena described in the first section of this book involve some kind of disturbance or disruption of the temporal order of things – in other words, the flow of *time* appears to be disrupted. But what exactly *is* time? We like to think that we know the answer: it is 'something' that gets ticked away by a clock. And, for many of us, there never seems to be enough of it. Since we equate the passage of time with the observed flow of events, we could argue that time is simply the *order* in which events are observed. This would *almost* pass as a working definition of time, except that it ignores the finiteness of the speed of light. When we look at the star Sirius, for example, we are seeing it as it was eight years ago, since that is how long it took the light from that star to reach us here on the earth. So how should we define 'now' on Sirius?

To complicate matters further, Einstein tells us that, from the point of view of an astronaut whizzing past the earth, in the direction of Sirius, 'now' on Sirius will be different from what it 'should' be from the perspective of a 'stationary' observer on the earth. Thus 'now' in distant parts of the universe is different for different observers, depending upon how they are moving in space.

Time Measurement

Since ticking clocks are, arguably, the most obvious manifestation of the passing of time, it is appropriate to consider here how time is measured. Our sense of the passing of time originated from observations of the movement of the heavenly bodies: of the rising and setting of the sun, of the phases of the moon, and of the seasonal cycle. For many centuries, these observations were sufficient for the regulation of daily affairs. However, as the pace of living began to speed up, mechanical clocks were developed, which measured the passage of time more accurately, either by the swing of a pendulum or by the oscillations of a balance wheel. Later, in the earlier part of the twentieth century, quartz clocks, and various 'atomic' clocks (including the ammonia clock and the caesium clock) were developed, principally for the purpose of accurate astronomical observations. But then, something odd was discovered: it was found that atomic clocks don't always agree precisely with mechanical clocks or, for that matter, with the earth's rotation as a timekeeper. It would appear, on the face of it, that the observed rate of the flow of time depends at least partly upon the choice of timekeeping device. For practical purposes, astronomers and physicists have adopted the caesium clock as standard, even though this necessarily entails the addition of an occasional 'leap second' at the end of the day, to compensate for changes in the earth's rate of spin.

(A somewhat similar situation occurs with regard to the measurement of temperature. The constant volume gas thermometer has been adopted as standard for temperature measurement, but the platinum resistance thermometer registers only 47°C when the gas thermometer registers 50°C.)

So the flow of time appears not to be as steady and dependable as we would like to think: it depends at least partly on what we are using for a clock. And when we take into account our own subjective perceptions of the flow of time, the situation becomes even more confused. Einstein once jokingly said, 'If you make love to a pretty girl for three hours, it seems like three minutes; but if you sit on a hot stove for three minutes, it seems like three hours.' So the *apparent* speed of the passage of time depends as much on one's mood as it does on physical factors.

Indeed, our perception of the 'speed' of the passing of time is strongly influenced by our own metabolic rate. As we grow older and our metabolic rate slows down, time seems to speed up. Many animals (including domestic cats and dogs) have a much faster metabolic rate than we do, and so ten or twelve years probably seem as long to them as seventy years do for us.

There are a number of fundamental questions which we may ask regarding the nature of time:

- What would it be like if time ran backwards?
- Does time have a beginning and/or an end? Is it infinite? Or again, is it cyclic?
- Is there more than one dimension of time?
- Do the past, present and future simultaneously co-exist?
- Is the flow of time smooth and continuous, or is it jerky?
- How long is 'now'?
- Is time travel possible?

Time's Arrow

Time is unique among the dimensions in that it perpetually and relentlessly flows in one direction only. Physicists call this *time's arrow*, and this is closely linked to the famous (or infamous) second law of thermodynamics. Stated in its simplest form, this law says that heat can never flow from a colder body or region to a hotter one; it can only go the other way. Cups of tea that have gone cold do not spontaneously warm up again. Everyone knows this. All of this sounds very straightforward and mundane – until we consider what would happen if time were to run backwards.

In this scenario, heat *would* flow from cold bodies to hotter ones. Cups of cold tea *would* spontaneously warm up on their own. Also, collapsed buildings would miraculously rise up out of piles of rubble and reassemble themselves. If this sounds strange, it gets even stranger. We would all be walking backwards, being careful to watch where we had just been, not where we were going. Animals would do the same. Fish would swim backwards and birds would fly backwards. Aircraft would take off and land backwards – almost certainly an impossible aerodynamic feat! And we would remember our 'future' but know nothing about our 'past'.

Baths would fill up from the plughole, with the water defying gravity and rising from the drains. The water in the bath would then separate itself into hot and cold and would again defy gravity by rising up and disappearing into the hot and cold taps.

Even stranger, our eyes would shine like car headlights, as light would be leaving them instead of entering them. And the sun would be a big black hole in the sky, absorbing radiation instead of giving it out.

The passage of time is thus a definite one-way ticket. The question is *do the laws of physics dictate that time should behave in this way?* Or is it something to do with our own *perceptions* of the flow of time? We shall return to this question later.

And yet, paradoxically, the pull of gravity would still be down, and not up. A projectile fired into the air will slow down as it goes up and speed up as it comes down, regardless of whether time is running forwards or backwards. And if we were to observe planets orbiting around a star, we would have no way of telling whether time was running forwards or backwards.

Time's Geometry

Did time have a beginning? And will it have an end? Or is it eternal, going on for ever – having already gone on for ever? Or again, does it follow a cyclic pattern, endlessly repeating itself – and history?

Cosmologists have observed that the light from distant galaxies is shifted toward the red end of the spectrum, and have assumed that this is a Doppler shift caused by the universe expanding. From this evidence, they have surmised that the universe must have 'exploded' from a single point some fourteen thousand million years ago (the 'Big Bang'), and that nothing at all happened before then. This, however, begs the question of what *caused* the Big Bang in the first instance.

There is a further complicating factor: the *rate* at which the universe is expanding is said to be increasing – which somehow seems inconsistent with the idea of the universe suddenly emerging from a single point.

An alternative model could be that the universe has followed a continuous exponential expansion. This would imply, however, that the 'Big Bang' was, in fact, a very gradual emergence from nothing, having occurred an infinitely long time ago. This does not tally with the scientists' calculation that the 'age' of the universe is only 14 thousand million years.

A more credible scenario is that the universe periodically expands and contracts, following a sine wave, and that its most recent 'bounce' from a minimum radius took place around 14 thousand million years ago. This, at least, concurs with the calculated 'age' of the universe.

So far, we have only looked at models in which time is 'rectilinear' – having just one dimension, regardless of whether it is finite or infinite. But Stephen Hawking has recently suggested that there could also be an 'imaginary' time – effectively a second dimension of time. A cyclic time model would be consistent with this approach.

The cyclic time scenario is an interesting one. Most modern scientists reject it, but it is compatible with the 'Big Bounce' model and so, maybe, cannot be readily dismissed. The ancient Greeks believed time to be cyclic, but they got the scaling wrong. They thought that time would repeat after only 24,000 years (approximately the period of the earth's precession), which they called the Great Year. Of course, time could not possibly repeat within such a short period, but if we allow no upper limit to how long it could be, then the cyclic time model does gain some credibility.

Some scientists, notably Sir Roger Penrose, have suggested that the universe may have been spawned from an earlier one, which would imply that there was a time before the Big Bang. In his book *Cycles of Time* he envisages an endless cycle of universes, each being spawned from its predecessor.

If time is *strictly* cyclic, then the history of the universe will be repeated *exactly* with the completion of every cycle. The sun and its planets – including the earth – will be re-created in exact detail on completion of every cycle. Animals and humans will once more appear on the earth, and all of human history will be repeated exactly as before. This may seem an incredible scenario, but it is not an impossible one.

There is, of course, the question of the second law of thermo-dynamics which, as we saw, states that heat cannot flow from a cold region to a hotter one. It is about the redistribution of energy such that, eventually, the energy is evenly distributed throughout the whole universe. In a cyclic time scenario, something would have to 'reset the clock' in this instance.

Going back to the notion of time having at least one extra dimension, the author J W Dunne, in his book *An Experiment with Time* (Chapter 1, Case 10) suggested that time could actually consist of an infinite number of dimensions, each of which would provide a yardstick against which the previous dimension could be measured. The principle of Occam's Razor, however, states that the simplest explanation for anything is likely to be the right one. On this count an infinite number of extra dimensions would seem superfluous. (But then again, what exactly do we mean by a 'dimension'?)

Time and Space

By the end of the nineteenth century, physicists thought that they had already discovered virtually all there was to know about the laws of physics. They were convinced that there would be little left for future generations of scientists to discover. As it appeared, there were only two 'loose ends' that remained to be cleared up. One of these was the mundane fact that a body that was heated until it was slightly incandescent glowed red. Why *red?* I shall have more to say on this in the next chapter.

The other anomaly was the result of the famous Michelson-Morley experiment, which was carried out in the early 1880s and reported on in 1887. It was known from earlier experiments that light travelled at a finite speed, and this speed had already been measured. It was thought, however, that light travelled through an invisible substance which they called the 'ether', and the aim of Michelson-Morley experiment was to measure the speed at which the earth travelled through this ether, as it orbited around the sun. But the result was unexpected: it appeared that the earth remained stationary within the ether, regardless of where it might be in its orbit. It was thus inferred that the speed of light must be same from the point of view of *every* observer, however they were moving in space.

To illustrate this point, let us consider a young boy travelling down a street on a skateboard at, say, ten miles per hour. He throws a stone forward, also at ten miles per hour. The speed of the stone relative to the ground is thus ten plus ten, which is twenty miles per hour. Common sense says this. But if, instead of throwing a stone, he shines an electric torch, pointing the beam straight ahead, the speed of the light relative to the ground is the *same* as the speed at which it leaves the torch. This is contrary to common sense, and it left the scientists puzzled.

It was this discovery that led Albert Einstein to formulate his Special Theory of Relativity, which he published in 1905. He predicted that if any moving body having mass approached the speed of light, it would become foreshortened in the direction of travel, its mass would increase dramatically and – most bizarrely of all – its time would slow down. Such a body could never actually reach the speed of light because it would then have zero length (or thickness), infinite mass (thus requiring an infinite energy input) and it would be completely stopped in time. On this account, the speed of light represents an upper limit to how fast any material object can travel. Time and space are thus very strange entities in that they are at least partly interchangeable – which led Einstein to combine them into a single entity which he called *spacetime*.

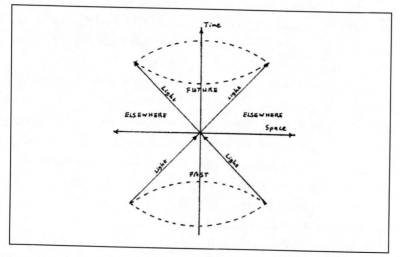

Fig. 6: Light Cones

To clarify this point, we may visualize this 'block universe' as a three-dimensional diagram showing the time axis (pointing upward) and two of the three dimensions of space (Fig. 6). Because of the finiteness of the speed of light, the diagram can be subdivided into a pair of *light cones* – a double cone in which the lower one represents the 'absolute past' and the upper one represents the 'absolute future' (from the perspective of an observer at the centre of the graph). The region outside the cones is 'elsewhere' – where events may or may not occur simultaneously, depending upon the observer's viewpoint.

As an illustration, let us suppose that George is sitting at home (being a home-loving earthling) while Astronaut Annie zooms past him, overhead. Let us suppose also that event A caused event B to happen, thus preceding it chronologically. In the block universe there will be an event C which is simultaneous with event A from George's viewpoint, but which is simultaneous with event B as seen by Annie.

Some eleven years later, Einstein expanded on his relativity theories, observing that the acceleration due to a propulsive force was indistinguishable from that due to gravitation. He concluded that the presence of a large mass in space, distorts the spacetime in its vicinity, and that time runs more slowly in such regions.

One effect of this is the phenomenon of *gravitational lensing* whereby the curvature of space around a massive body causes the light from a more distant body to curve around the nearer one. (One might thus expect the image of the more distant body to appear as a 'halo' around the nearer one – but this is not necessarily what happens. Instead, the nearer body is surrounded by *four* images of the more distant body – a phenomenon known as the *Einstein cross*. More on this later.)

Bizarre as it sounds, the time dilation effect is real. Evidence of this comes from the fact that mu mesons, particles which have such a short life that they ought never to be able to reach the earth from outer space, actually do so in large numbers. Because they travel so fast, the time dilation effect affords them a longer life than they would have otherwise. It should be noted also that, satellite navigation systems would not work properly if they did not compensate for time dilation, as this would result in a cumulative error in the geographic positions thus given.

Is Time Continuous?

We normally think of both space and time as being smooth and continuous. After all, this *appears* to be the case. But what if they are not? In the 1960s, a Russian physicist (Andrei Sakharov?) suggested that both space and time might be *quantized* – time being jerky like an old movie film, and space being grainy. He suggested also that these 'grains of space' might be arranged in a simple cubic lattice, similar to a sodium chloride crystal. (The 'Einstein cross' appears to provide evidence of this.) He arrived at these conclusions following a study of particle physics, in which it had become evident that spinning particles such as electrons can only orient themselves in certain discrete directions. The length of a 'grain' of space is known as the Planck length (after the German physicist Max Planck), and can be calculated using the formula:

$$length = \sqrt{(Gh/c^3)}$$

where G is Newton's gravitational constant, h is Planck's constant and c is the speed of light. This length is approximately 10^{-35} metres – much too small to be observed directly, even using instrumentation. (To put these numbers into perspective, if we imagine the hydrogen atom expanded to a radius of one billion (10^9) light years, the Planck length scaled up *pro rata* would be about the length of my back garden in Banbury. It is not a big garden.)

The 'chronon' or Planck time is the time it would take for light to travel the distance of one Planck length and is approximately 10^{-43} seconds. Again, this is such a small interval of time that it can never be observed directly – hence the everyday illusion of the 'smoothness' of time and space. Indeed, the chronon is so small that there are more chronons in a one-second interval than there are seconds in the present age of the universe.

(In the next chapter we shall examine the history and development of quantum theory, and we will see further evidence that both time and space have this granulated property, rather than them being smooth and continuous.)

How Long is 'Now'?

We commonly think of 'now' as an extremely thin sliver of time, separating the past (which we remember) from the future (about which we can only speculate). We think also that among the past, present and future, only 'now' is real. And, from the previous section, we would infer that 'now' ought to be of at least one chronon in duration.

Recent research, notably by Marc Wittmann, suggests that our perception of 'now' and, indeed the flow of time itself, is a function of how the brain processes incoming information, and that this has a duration of some 2–3 seconds. Our perception of the present typically goes through a three-phase cycle which begins with a *functional moment*, lasting only milliseconds, in which the brain makes its immediate response to incoming stimuli. This is followed by the *experienced moment*, lasting 2–3 seconds, when the mind becomes consciously aware of the stimulus the brain has received. As this cycle repeats, it takes the mind some 30 seconds to appreciate the continuity of the flow of time.

People who meditate are often able to expand the 2–3 second phase, sometimes to six – or even eight – seconds. Such people tend to perceive time as passing more slowly, and commonly claim a heightened awareness of events around them.

In the light of this research , it becomes evident that 'now' is, at best, a fuzzy concept and, it would seem, this fuzziness must apply also to reality itself.

Is Time Travel Possible?

Common sense would say a resounding *no* to this question. However, as we have just seen, there is evidence that time is discontinuous at the quantum level. Does this mean – in exceptional cases, at least – that larger discontinuities in the flow of time are possible? The answer to this, it would appear, has to be 'maybe'. Some scientists now think this, the reason for their line of thinking coming from the study of *Black Holes*.

A Black Hole is, in theory, a point in space having a finite mass but zero size – and hence an infinite density. Such a point is called a *singularity*. Black Holes generally result from the collapse of super-massive stars that have reached the end of their life cycle, and whose gravity is too strong to prevent the collapse of the star to a single point. In practice, however, the Planck length (10^{-35} metres) represents the smallest region of space that any mass could occupy, and this is not a zero length. There is a further factor also: *everything* out there in space – galaxies – stars – planets – and moons – is spinning. Why should Black Holes be any different? And spinning Black Holes do not have a singularity at their centre; instead they have a vortex. (Water draining down a plughole is a perfect analogy of this.) According to some theories, Black Hole vortices can link up across time and space to form *wormholes* – portals to other places – and to other times.

Travel into the future is of little consequence as we are steadily doing it all the time. But, as Einstein tells us, the rate of travel can be faster or slower. Travel into the past, however, raises some interesting paradoxes. One can imagine a scenario in which one travels into the past and murders one's own mother while she was just a little girl. In this case, one could not have been born, and so could not have committed the murder. An impossible scenario. Many scientists take this as evidence that time travel into the past is impossible. However, the jury is still out.

There is a recorded incident in which the famous physicist Nikola Tesla stood inside a powerful rotating magnetic field and experienced what, to him, seemed like a 'timeless' state. The details are somewhat obscure, however, and we cannot say for certain that this was a genuine case of time travel.

Probably the most notable proposition on time travel is the one put forward by Frank Tipler. He suggests that, given a vast amount of energy, it may be possible to create a cylindrical vortex of very dense matter which would act as a gravity well. (This sounds like the spinning Black Hole again.) Such an arrangement has been dubbed a *Tipler cylinder*. Needless to say, there has never been one created.

A curious case involving a claim about time travel is that of someone calling himself John Titor, who, in 2000, claimed to be a time traveller from the year 2036. He gave some technical details of the machine which he had supposedly used, and also gave an account of some events which he 'remembered' from 2036. These included a civil war in the USA, starting in 2005 (which didn't happen) and also a war in 2015 which would kill three billion people. As of September 2015, this also hasn't happened – it seems that he was wrong about this, also.

John Titor (whoever he was) disappeared from public view as suddenly and mysteriously as he had appeared. I am open-minded but, given his dubious track record, I suspect a hoax.

Is Time Real?

This may seem a strange question to ask, but we have already seen that, as a corollary of Einstein's theory, the past, present and future could all coexist as a 'timeless' state (the 'block universe'). The implication of this must be that everything is predetermined and that we do not possess the free will that would enable us to change any of it. This does raise the question of why we experience a succession of events, rather than everything all happening at once. It also raises the question of why the block universe should be configured the way it is.

Three quantum physicists, John Wheeler, Bryce De Witt and Peter Bergmann, in the 1960s, tried applying a quantum mechanical model to the universe as a whole. They derived a complicated equation (now known as the Wheeler-De Witt equation) in which time did not figure at all. Another physicist, Julian Barbour, has expanded on this. He says that nothing exists except pure *moments* in time. He claims that our sense of the passage of time is illusory, and that our sense of 'before' arises purely because we have *remembered* it. He claims that causality does not exist, and that this is a static universe in which nothing ever happens – except that we experience a succession of 'moments'.

This, essentially, is the 'block universe' model again, in which everything is pre-ordained and time is, effectively, a fourth dimension of space. It is a universe in which past, present and future all co-exist – *including the past, present and future states of our own bodies.*

But this is not how we perceive the universe. If this model is correct, then 'we' must be entities distinct from our bodies, travelling through space and time along a trajectory defined by our bodies – like trains travelling along a railway track. We do not perceive everything 'all at once'; we perceive things sequentially. Our perception, rightly or wrongly, is that the universe *unfolds* itself, and that we do have at least *some* power to influence the course of events.

In the block universe, we are 'something' that transcends both time and space, observing things only a bit at a time. Conversely, time is something we manufacture in our own minds as we observe everything and exercise our free will. Time is thus very much tied up with the observer; it is not so much a dimension as the trajectory taken by the observer through the four-dimensional spacetime.

So What is Time?

Whatever the laws of physics may say, we perceive the passage of time as a succession of observed events, and we measure it using clocks and calendars. The findings of modern physics indicate that time is malleable, flowing at different rates for different observers and in different locations, and that the sequence of events is not necessarily the same for every observer. There is evidence that time may be jerky, rather than continuous, and a possibility – which cannot be lightly dismissed – that it may even repeat itself over a very long period. We know also, from recent research, that 'now' is a fuzzy entity, of finite duration, but dependent upon the perceptions of the observer. And, to cap it all, there are physicists who claim that time isn't even real!

6: The Pixellated Universe

The universe is indeed a strange place. Einstein has shown us that the laws of physics are not quite as we would expect. Time and space are malleable and at least partly interchangeable. Energy and matter also are interchangeable, as was shown in Einstein's famous equation:

$$E = mc^2$$

If all of this sounds strange, things are about to become even stranger. In the previous chapter we saw that there were some 'loose ends' to nineteenth century classical physics which could not be explained. The anomalous result of the Michelson-Morley was one of them, which, as we have seen, led Einstein to formulate his theories of relativity. We turn now to the other anomaly which classical physics was unable to explain, namely, the fact that a slightly incandescent body glows a dull red colour. The question was, why *red*? Why not white – or blue – or green, for that matter?

The phenomenon is known in physics as *black body radiation*, since a body which is perfectly black completely absorbs all wavelengths of light. But when heated to incandescence, the colour of the glow will change with increasing temperature from red, to yellow and finally to white. The sun, paradoxically, is an almost perfect 'black body' – except that it doesn't look black because it is so hot. If the sun were cold, it would be almost jet black.

It was the German physicist Max Planck who, in 1900, first proffered an explanation for the colour changes manifested in black body radiation. He suggested that, instead of being emitted continuously, the excess energy from a hot body was emitted in little chunks – which he called *quanta* (from the Latin *quantum*, meaning a 'little bundle'). He suggested that the energy of each quantum of radiation was related to its frequency of vibration, as given in the formula:

$$E = h\nu$$

where h is the constant we now refer to as Planck's constant, and ν (the Greek letter 'nu') represents the frequency of vibration, given in cycles per second. Planck himself was very conservative in outlook and actually disliked the idea he was proposing. He did not seriously believe that energy could be emitted in little chunks, and regarded this as merely an intellectual ruse to try to find an explanation for the colour changes. Modern quantum physicists, however, accept that Planck's suggestion was right all along, and have been working on its ramifications ever since. Even as I write, quantum theory is still a work in progress, but I will outline the main developments that have taken place since Planck's day.

First, however, I will make the point that the mass of any elementary particle can be equated with a specific vibrational frequency by combining Planck's equation with Einstein's equation. Thus:

$$mc^2 = h\nu$$
$$or\ m = (h/c^2)\nu$$

Every elementary particle accordingly has its own characteristic frequency of vibration, dependent upon its mass. Conversely, a photon (a 'particle' of light) has a notional 'mass' which can be calculated from its frequency of vibration. Since blue light has a faster vibration than red light, it follows that blue photons 'weigh' more than red ones do.

One important ramification of Planck's theory is that we cannot know the precise values of both the position (x) and the momentum (p) of a particle. (Momentum is mass multiplied by velocity.) Thus, if Δx ('delta x') is the uncertainty in the position and Δp is the uncertainty in the momentum, the product $\Delta x \Delta p$ must be at least as great as Planck's constant (h), if not greater. This is known as the *Heisenberg uncertainty principle*, named after Werner Heisenberg, who first proposed it in 1927. This uncertainty is intrinsic to the laws of physics, and cannot be circumvented in any way.

Another pioneer was the Count Louis de Broglie who suggested that the particles (electrons etc.) that compose matter can manifest as waves as well as particles. Even Einstein was shocked at this idea.

It is characteristic of elementary particles generally that their quantum properties (spin, momentum, etc.) cannot be known until these are observed and measured. Particles can also become *entangled* with one another, so that their quantum properties become interrelated and dependant on each other. This has the bizarre result that if we measure the quantum state of an entangled particle then the quantum state of its partner is instantly determined *even if the latter particle is at the far end of the universe*. Einstein again was horrified at this idea, calling it 'spooky action at a distance'. But in 1964, John Bell confirmed that the theory was correct, using the mathematical proof now referred to as *Bell's theorem*. (This result appears to contradict Einstein's prediction that simultaneity must be dependent on the observer.)

Quantum theory is rife with uncertainty and unpredictability. Every elementary 'particle' (including the photons, which make up light) is also a wave. Also, we can never be certain where they are. A particle can be anywhere – even in two or more places at once. It can also exist simultaneously in two states at once – a phenomenon known as *superposition*.

Erwin Schrödinger (another famous quantum physicist) once proposed a somewhat absurd scenario in which a cat was enclosed in a box where it could not be observed. Inside the box also was a hammer which would crack open a phial of poisonous gas if a particular radioactive atom decayed, thus killing the cat. His argument was that, in the absence of observation, and due to the random nature of radioactive decay, we could have no way of telling whether the cat was alive or dead, and so the cat itself would be in a state of superposition. The cat would (in theory) be alive and dead at the same time.

One thing we must never forget, however, is that animals are observers also, just like ourselves. And the laws of physics don't care what the species of the observer might be. Whether the observer happens to be a cat, a dog or a physicist ought to make no difference at all. The cat itself will therefore know if it is still alive in the box, even if we don't.

Schrödinger is also best known for a somewhat abstruse equation which he developed for quantum physics. The English physicist Paul Dirac elaborated on it further. Dirac's most significant contribution, however, was the discovery (through theoretical reasoning) of *antimatter*. Antimatter has the strange property that it annihilates ordinary matter if the two come into contact with each other – releasing vast amounts of energy, according to Einstein's equation. Dirac envisaged a 'sea' of particles in which, if a particle were removed from its regular position, it would (in effect) sit on top of the 'sea' and be perceived as 'matter', while the gap left behind would be perceived as a 'particle' of antimatter.

The Particle Zoo

Over the decades, with more than a little help from quantum theory, physicists have evolved a classification of elementary particles, which they call the *Standard Model*. There are more than a dozen particles thus classified, including the renowned Higgs boson, whose existence is now confirmed from experiments with the Large Hadron Collider. Only a small handful of particles make up ordinary matter, however, namely the proton, the neutron and the electron. Protons and neutrons, in turn, are now known to be made up from even smaller components known as *quarks*. (I refer to quarks as 'components' rather than 'particles' as it appears that they cannot exist as independent entities on their own.)

Of particular interest here are the *neutrinos*, particles having only a negligible mass and no electric charge. At one time, neutrinos were thought to have zero mass as well as zero charge – but this would effectively make them particles of nothing. And I do not believe that there can be such a thing as particles of nothing. There are, in fact, three types of neutrino: the electron neutrino, the mu neutrino and the tau neutrino. There is evidence that any neutrino can spontaneously transmute into either of the other two types.

Bearing in mind the 'block universe' model described in the previous chapter, it follows that every elementary particle should have its own trajectory in spacetime. The renowned physicist Richard P Feynman utilized this idea to construct a series of diagrams – now known as *Feynman diagrams* – which not only illustrate the particles' trajectories, but also show how the different types of particle interact with one another to form new particles.

Because only a small number of types of particle make up ordinary matter as we know it, it raises the question: what is the function (if any) of all the other particles? Many of these particles can only exist for tiny fractions of a second before decaying into other particles, and so it hardly makes sense to speak of them having a 'function'. But it is legitimate to enquire why such ephemeral particles should have any existence at all.

But, perhaps, we ought not to dismiss the possibility that there may be worlds elsewhere that are composed of some of these other particles. It may even turn out, eventually, that the 'spirit world', as perceived by psychics, is simply a parallel world made from some of the finer particles – neutrinos being a strong candidate in this instance.

Quantum Gravity

One difficulty that physicists have been grappling with over many years is the apparent disconnection between the worlds of the very large (as expressed through Einstein's theories of relativity) and the very small (as expressed through quantum theory). Both theories work superbly well in their own domains – there's plenty of experimental evidence to confirm this. But the ends don't meet. In particular, quantum theory cannot explain gravity.

This is an ongoing area of research, however. One product of this has been *string theory*, in which it is proposed that every elementary particle is really a very tiny vibrating 'string' – somewhat analogous to a violin or guitar string. The proponents of string theory say that the universe must have ten dimensions – the four dimensions of spacetime plus six others which are deemed to be 'rolled up very small'. There are five different versions of string theory, however, each of them slightly different. And there is no universal agreement on which of them (if any) is correct.

In 1995, at the String Theory Conference at the University of Southern California, Edward Witten suggested that the various string theories might be combined into a single, over-arching theory, which he called M-theory. (It is uncertain what the 'M' stands for in this nomenclature.) M-theory replaces the idea of 'strings' with one of multidimensional 'membranes' – which have been dubbed *branes*. This theory also proposes *eleven* dimensions, rather than the ten proposed under the string theories. To the best of my knowledge, however, M-theory has never been properly formulated, and is still a work in progress.

An alternative model – and the one that I would endorse – is known as *loop quantum gravity* (LQG). LQG agrees with Andrei

Sakharov's suggestion that space and time might themselves be quantized (grainy or *pixellated*), which we discussed in the previous chapter. LQG, however, does not necessarily confirm (nor does it rule out) the possibility that the 'grains of space' might be arranged in a cubic lattice. Like M-theory before it, LQG proposes a universe of eleven dimensions, rather than the ten proposed in the string theories.

An eleven-dimensional universe is interesting mathematically as it gives us *one* dimension of time, *three* of space and *seven* of 'something else'. The numbers 1, 3 and 7 are all of the order:

$$2^n - 1$$

Thus, if we eventually find that even eleven dimensions are not enough, then we will need to add a further *fifteen* dimensions, bringing the total up to 26.

Quantum Space

If space is quantized or pixellated according to Sakharov's model (and LQG) then this has some interesting ramifications. One implication is that space, far from being the 'nothing' we generally think it is, actually behaves like a slightly viscous fluid. The space surrounding a spinning object is actually pulled around as the object spins – a phenomenon known as *frame dragging*. This can be demonstrated using an apparatus in which a laser beam is split in such a way that its two branches graze the top and bottom of a flywheel. When the flywheel is spun at a high speed, one branch of the light beam is speeded up but the other is slowed down. This introduces a phase difference between the two components of the beam, when they are re-combined, which registers as a reduction in the light intensity. This can then be detected using a light meter. The whole apparatus has to be sealed in a vacuum to demonstrate that it is the actual *space* that is being pulled around, and not air.

So-called 'empty' space also exerts a small, but measurable pressure on all physical objects placed within it – an effect known as the *Casimir effect* (named after the Dutch physicist, Hendrik Casimir). This can be demonstrated using a pair of parallel metal plates, which are earthed to eliminate any electro-static effects. Again, the apparatus has to be enclosed in a vacuum chamber to eliminate the effects of atmospheric pressure. Provided that the plates are sufficiently close together, they will move toward each other – the explanation being that, since there is less space in the gap than outside, the larger volume of space outside will exert the greater pressure.

A further implication is that space (or spacetime) must be similar to a loosely woven dishcloth. We know that if we push a knitting needle (or a pencil) into the cloth, this will open up 'fault lines' in the fabric as the threads are pushed aside. We know from special relativity that the presence of a large mass distorts the surrounding space, effectively puckering it up. If the space is also pixellated, then this is equivalent to the knitting needle being pushed into the dishcloth generating similar 'fault lines' in the fabric of space itself. The largest (most massive) objects in space are, of course, the heavenly bodies – including Jupiter, the moon, and the like. If these bodies are generating fault lines in space then, when these bodies reach certain positions, the fault lines will become aligned with one another – which could possibly cause some minimal, but perceptible, disruption to radio signals, and the like. This could provide a possible physical basis for the claim, long made by traditional astrologers, that planets spaced at multiples of 90 degrees, as seen from the earth, have a generally adverse or destabilizing influence.

Pixellated space could also explain another feature of astrology – the twelve signs of the zodiac. The geometry of the circle is such that when superimposed on a 4x4 square matrix, the circle is divided into twelve equal arc-lengths. Pixellated space could provide an actual physical basis for this. (We shall examine this idea further in Chapter 13.)

Quantum Chess

The game of chess offers an excellent analogy to the behaviour of quantum particles. The locations (and other properties) of quantum particles can only be known when they are actually *observed*. When unobserved, the particles could be anywhere and in any state. Similarly, the positions of pieces on a chessboard are only determined between moves. The reason for this is that, while the rules of the game determine where the pieces can move to, they do not specify the actual *trajectories* of the pieces. This point is most strongly illustrated by the Knight's move. Most people describe the Knight's move as being two squares orthogonally (parallel to the sides of the board) and then one square at right angles to this. However, this move can also be described as one square orthogonally followed by one diagonally. Again, we may argue that the Knight follows a beeline to its destination, squeezing in between other pieces, if necessary – which would explain why the Knight is allowed to 'jump' over other pieces. Which one of these descriptions of the Knight's move is correct? The answer is, *all of them are*.

The analogy may be carried further, since no piece is ever perfectly centred within its square on the board. The rules also do not specify which direction the Knight should be facing, and pieces which, theoretically, travel in straight lines are often picked up and then plonked down again on a new square. Actual games of chess thus always confer an element of uncertainty over the exact placement of pieces on the board – an uncertainty that the rules of the game can never eliminate. Just like quantum mechanics!

Parallel Universes

We saw earlier that elementary particles have a bizarre property in that they can sometimes behave like particles, and sometimes like waves. One of the odd results of this is that if we fire a stream of particles through a pair of double slits, they will produce an interference pattern on a screen placed behind the slits. Even an individual particle can evidently pass through both slits at once and interfere with itself. One interpretation of this is that, in its 'wave' state the 'particle' is really a *collection* of particles forming a 'probability wave'. Or, alternatively, it is still a single particle, but in several places at once.

To try to get around this difficulty, Hugh Everett, in 1957, proposed that this could make sense if we supposed that the particle were to occupy different positions in different *universes*. Some of these universes could be similar to our own, but others could be very different. And, according to this model, not all universes need necessarily be inhabited by living beings.

If this model is indeed correct, then our own universe would simply be one of many within a *multiverse*.

The Anthropic Principle

Before I leave this chapter, I must draw the reader's attention to something which, on reflection, appears even stranger than either relativity or quantum theory. It appears that our universe has been 'fine-tuned' to make the life process (and ourselves) possible. Many of the physical constants would need to differ by only a very small amount for life to become *im*possible. To give an example: if the electrical charge on an electron were only slightly more than its present value, then the valency electrons of atoms would be so tightly bound to those atoms that there could not be any chemical reactions – and there would be no life process. However, if the electronic charge were only slightly smaller, then the valency electrons (and possibly other electrons also) would drift away from their host atoms, again rendering chemical processes impossible. It almost looks as if something – or someone – *chose* to design a universe in which life would be possible. This is known in physics as the *Anthropic Principle*.

Even Richard Feynman, one of the greatest quantum physicists of all time, was forced to admit: 'Nobody really understands quantum theory'. He used to tell his students: 'It's no use asking me how things can possibly be like that – because, the truth is, *nobody* knows how it can possibly be like that'. Much of quantum theory mathematics is so fiendishly complicated that even I, as a scientist, find it challenging. (But I didn't need the maths to write this book.) I think the wave-particle conundrum may be best understood if we can visualize it in terms of knots and ripples in the fabric of spacetime itself. If this is the case, however, then we will really need *two* spacetimes, each superimposed on the other. One of these will then be the spacetime that gets distorted by the presence of matter, while the other serves as a 'reference' spacetime against which the distortions of the first one can be measured.

An underlying issue of fundamental importance is the role of the *observer* in both relativity and quantum mechanics. There is evidence that we, as observers, have some influence over what happens at the quantum level, and it makes a significant difference to the behaviour of quantum particles when they are observed – a topic we shall return to, later. A big unanswered question, however, is *what, if anything, can explain the phenomenon of conscious awareness?* We shall examine this question further in the next chapter.

7: Brains, Computers and Consciousness

We have seen in the previous two chapters that the role of the observer is important – but what exactly *is* an observer? Is it just people – or does it include animals also? And what of plants? Do they also have a rudimentary level of awareness? After all, they too are classed as living things. Some might even argue that so-called 'inanimate' matter may itself have a very primitive level of awareness, even more rudimentary than that of plants.

It will be instructive here to examine the structure and functioning of neural systems, with a particular emphasis on the mammalian brain. Before we can do this, however, we need to bear in mind that neural activity is essentially an *electrical* phenomenon, and that water plays a major role, also. We will begin therefore by looking at the phenomena of electricity and magnetism.

Electricity and Magnetism

Since Michael Faraday discovered the link between electricity and magnetism in the early nineteenth century, we have learned a lot about the nature of electrical and magnetic phenomena – including the fact that light itself is the result of oscillating electric and magnetic fields. But what exactly *is* electricity? What exactly do we mean by an 'electric charge'? The truth is that we don't really know – except that it is something different from mass. But again, we don't know what mass is, either. We do know that electric charges can repel as well as attract one another – something which mass cannot do. Despite our ignorance, however, we have capitalized upon the behaviour of electrical and magnetic systems in a big way. First it was the electric light and the electric motor; then we had the radio, followed soon after by television. And now, today, we have computers which not only perform number-crunching (hence the name) but can, to some extent, even mimic some of the abilities of the human brain. We shall examine this topic shortly.

Nature's Oddity: the Water Molecule

The most abundant chemical compound in the universe is water (hydrogen being the most abundant element). It surpasses both methane and ammonia in abundance, these being common on many other planets. The water molecule is one of nature's oddities, however. We all know from school chemistry that water has the chemical formula H_2O. What is less well known, however, is that the three atoms that make up the molecule are not arranged in a straight line. There is a 108-degree bend in the molecule. And, due to the distribution of electrons within it, the molecule is actually a small electric dipole – the electrical equivalent of a bar magnet. At ordinary temperatures, this property causes the water molecules to link up, forming long chains and other structures – which explains why water is a liquid at room temperature and not a gas. While this electrical property of liquid water is only peripheral to the subject of brain science, we should be aware that the presence of water (especially running water) can disturb the surrounding electrical and magnetic fields, and that this in turn can have implications for the functioning of the brain.

Neurons

Before we examine the architecture of the brain and nervous system, we need to be aware of how an individual neuron (nerve cell) actually 'works'. A typical neuron (Fig. 7) comprises a cell body (which contains the cell nucleus and mitochondria), a large number of branching filaments called *dendrites* and a long projection known as the *axon*. The axon also branches into filaments, which in turn engage with the dendrites of neighbouring cells at junctions known as *synapses*. Wrapped around the axon, are bundles of a substance known as *myelin*, forming a segmented sheath around the axon.

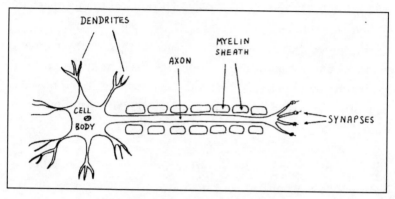

Fig.7: Structure of a Typical Neuron

The myelin sheath contains a reservoir of sodium ions, which, of course, are positively charged, giving the sheath itself an overall positive charge. The interior of the cell (including the axon) contains a supply of potassium ions, which again are positively charged – but the cell interior as a whole has a slight negative charge. Thus, in its 'resting' state, the neuron with its sheath forms a small electric battery.

When the neuron 'fires', sodium ions from the sheath permeate the cell wall, flooding part of the axon with sodium ions. This moves as a pulse of positive charge away from the cell body and toward the free end of the axon, and thence to the synapses. Potassium ions from the axon then cross the cell wall back into the myelin sheath to restore the resting potential.

As every physics student learns at school, wherever there is any movement of electric charges, this constitutes an electric *current* – and, as we know, this is *always* accompanied by a magnetic field. This is an important consideration in any study of the brain and nervous system, the implication being that the nervous system – and indeed the whole body – of any living being (human or animal) must necessarily be permeated by a scintillating matrix of electric and magnetic fields. The big question for consideration here is, *is this what some people might refer to as the 'etheric' or 'light' body?* The answer to this question, evidently, has to be 'yes'.

(If, under exceptional circumstances, this electromagnetic matrix is able temporarily to disengage itself from the physical brain and neural network, this could conceivably account for the 'out of body' excursions experienced by Sylvan Muldoon and Robert Monroe.)

Brain Structure

Neurons do not, of course, function in isolation. Especially in higher animals including ourselves – but also in many very primitive creatures – neurons are organized into networks in which they interact with one another. Thus when one neuron 'fires', its signal is relayed to one or more adjacent neurons via the synapses and the dendrites of those other neurons.

In terms of structural and functional complexity, the human brain (Fig. 8) is the supreme example of such a network. Other mammalian brains have virtually the same structure and functioning as a human brain, the only real difference being that they are generally smaller and somewhat less developed. This is especially the case with the cerebral hemispheres, which are much larger (in proportion to the rest of the brain) in humans than in other animals.

The human cerebrum also differs from that of other animals in the specialized use made of the left hemisphere, which is concerned principally with language, computation and logical reasoning. Wernicke's area (marked 'W' in Fig.8) is concerned with language comprehension, while Broca's area (marked 'B') controls speech production. Both of these areas are normally found in the left hemisphere only.

The human right hemisphere and (presumably) both hemispheres in other animal brains are more holistic in how they process information, and are concerned mainly with spatial

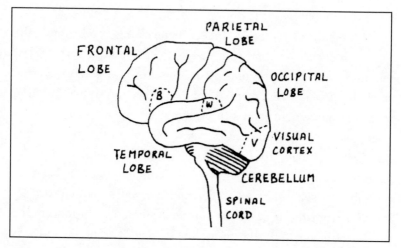

Fig. 8: The Human Brain (Left Side) – General View

location and emotional expression.

The lobes of the cerebrum are also specialized in their functioning. The frontal lobe is concerned with planning and decision-making, the parietal lobe governs motor movements, the occipital lobe is concerned with spatial awareness (and includes the visual cortex 'V'), while the temporal lobes are involved mainly with auditory processing, memory and (on the left side only) language comprehension and processing. Every part of the surface of the cerebrum has a highly specialized function – even down to the level of individual cells.

The cerebral hemispheres are connected to each other by a thick bundle of neurons known as the *corpus callosum*, which enables them to communicate directly with each other. Interestingly, in some patients, the corpus callosum has been surgically cut, as a radical treatment for severe epilepsy. This is known as a *split-brain operation*, and studies have been conducted to see how patients respond to this. It has been found that each hemisphere tends to behave like a separate brain in its own right, seemingly having a 'mind' of its own. This may manifest, for example, as the person's left hand trying to restrain the right hand from whatever it is doing.

At the back of the brain, tucked beneath the cerebrum, is the *cerebellum*. Like the cerebrum, it has deeply folded surface, but the folds are more regular than those of the cerebrum. The cerebellum plays an essential role in balancing and regulating muscular movements, smoothing them out.

Beneath the cerebrum and circling the top of the brainstem is the *limbic system*, the main components of which are the *hippocampus* (so named because its curved shape is said to resemble a seahorse) and the *olfactory bulbs,* which project forward from the base of the limbic system. The hippocampus plays a crucial role in the formation of new memories, and it is noted that London taxi drivers (renowned for their detailed knowledge of the capital's streets) nearly always have an enlarged hippocampus.

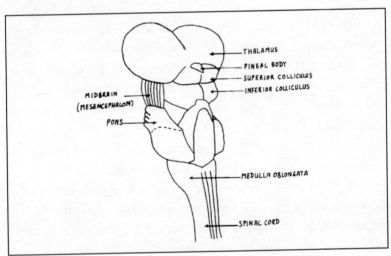

Fig. 9: The Human Brainstem – Left Rear View

The *Brainstem* (Fig. 9) is the column at the centre of the brain and continues downward to merge with the spinal cord. Structurally, it is much more complicated than the diagram indicates, and so I shall only refer to its principal features.

The Thalamus, at the top of the brainstem, has been likened a pair of walnuts in appearance, but is generally referred to as a single structure. Its main function is to process incoming sensory data before sending it on to the higher centres of the brain, thus acting as the brain's main 'relay station'.

The Pineal Body (also known as the pineal 'gland') is attached just below the thalamus, at the back. Descartes considered the pineal body to be the seat of the soul, since it is the only structure in the brain that is unpaired. The pineal has also been likened to a 'third eye' and, while its position within the mammalian brain doesn't allow it to function as such, it is known to be light-sensitive. It secretes a substance known as melatonin, which regulates the sleeping and waking cycle.

The Midbrain (known also as the mesencephalon) has functions to do with eye movement, body movement and hearing. Behind the midbrain are the *superior colliculus*, connected with vision, and the *inferior colliculus*, connected with hearing.

The Pons (meaning a 'bridge') is a bundle of nerve fibres serving as the main 'crossroads' in the brain. The cerebellum (omitted from the diagram for clarity) is attached at the back of the pons.

The brain thus has an overall 'vertical' organization starting from the *cortical level* (cerebrum and cerebellum) at the top, going down to the limbic level and thence to the upper and lower parts of the brainstem. The higher-level mental functions are concentrated in the cortical level, while the more basic functions (maintaining consciousness) are located in the lower centres. Indeed, the lowest part of the brain is sometimes referred to as the 'reptilian' brain.

The brains of lower animals (amphibians and reptiles, for example) are 'wired' differently from mammalian brains, and lack many of the 'higher' cortical structures – although these are usually still present at a rudimentary level. As a consequence of this different wiring, for example, many of these creatures are able to see movement, but cannot see a stationary object.

In behavioural terms, however, the apparent 'intelligence' demonstrated by any creature is determined not so much by its overall brain size as by its brain size in relation to the rest of the body. Thus, for example, crows (which have a small brain in absolute terms) have been observed to make and use tools – but then, their brains are relatively large compared to their body size.

The Malleable Brain

Through our brains, we continue day by day to build a catalogue of experience: memories, new skills, and the like. As we have seen, the hippocampus plays a vital role in laying down new memories.

We do actually have more than one kind of memory. We have a short-term memory for retaining facts that will only be needed for a few minutes (a telephone number, for example). If the same information is repeatedly held in the short-term memory, or if some event has a strong emotional impact, this then becomes translated into the long-term memory, in which case the hippocampus springs into action. (People with a damaged hippocampus have difficulty in forming new long-term memories.) Knowledge of languages, and also practical skills are further examples of the long-term memory at work.

What may be surprising to some people is that, as we develop new skills and memories, the brain's architecture is changed at cellular level. Neurons grow new dendrites and form new synapses, thus linking up with other neurons to which they were not linked before. Also, from early adulthood, many of our brain cells die off, reducing (or paring) the existing number of neural links and making the formation of new memories more difficult. (Exercise, good diet and doing brain puzzles are often promoted as means of countering this decline.)

The Seat of Consciousness?

The brain is indeed a complicated system of interrelated parts, each having its own particular function. And yet, as we go about our daily business of thinking, speaking and acting, we are completely unaware of the sheer complexity of the processes going on inside our heads. When I look at diagrams and models of the human brain, I have the impression of seeing the brain as an external object, even though I know that my own brain is very similar to what I'm seeing. We perceive ourselves as individual unitary entities rather than as systems of interacting neurons and other organs.

In this brief tour of the brain I have, for simplicity, omitted a great amount of detail. But the complexity of this organ and its structures is already evident. The big question is, *which part of the brain – if any – may properly be regarded as the true 'seat of consciousness'?*

On the face of it, the thalamus might seem an obvious choice. It is centrally positioned within the brain and has strong connections with most other parts. Activity within the reticular formation (located within the brainstem) is, however, essential for maintaining a state of alertness. If the reticular formation shuts down, then the person loses consciousness. Also, there is the question of where our memories are located. The thalamus is obviously too small for this. Again, when I reflect on everything I know and everything that I can remember from past experience, I am overwhelmed by the sheer *vastness* of this bank of information. Nowhere in the brain seems 'big enough' to store all this knowledge. If it is simply stored away 'somewhere' in the physical brain, this is like all the books in the Library of Congress being stashed away in a garden shed! It would therefore seem more likely that the physical brain (and the thalamus, in particular) operates somewhat like a smart mobile phone, which retrieves the information from 'elsewhere' rather than simply storing it.

Considering that many functions are distributed across the brain (due to its internal connections) it appears unlikely that there is a definitive 'seat of consciousness' anywhere in the brain. The thalamus, due to its central position, continues to be the most likely candidate for one – but it would seem that this is somewhere *around* the thalamus rather than in it. Again, we must not forget Professor Lorber's mathematics student (Chapter 1, Case 23) who had virtually no physical brain at all. Where was *his* seat of consciousness?

Can Machines Think?

The development of electronic computers has prompted many people to liken the performance of such machines to the workings of the human brain. Indeed, computers have sometimes been referred to as 'electronic brains'. Computers work differently from the brain, however. Their hardware is different, as is the way in which they process information.

The early precursors of computers were simple calculating devices such as Napier's bones, logarithm tables, the abacus and the slide rule. These are all simple mechanical devices, and can in no way be likened to the brain, either in structure or mode of operation. Blaise Pascal, Gottfried Leibnitz and Charles Babbage all subsequently designed and built more sophisticated mechanical devices for performing calculations, but these again were mere number-crunching machines which bore no resemblance to the human brain. Then, in 1936, Alan Turing proposed that large and complex calculations could be performed very rapidly by breaking them down into simple steps, which could then be executed by a machine. John von Neumann expanded on this idea, proposing that such a machine could run automatically using a set of stored instructions.

The earliest electronic computers were built in the 1940s and, since transistors had not yet been invented, they had to be constructed using radio valves (known as 'vacuum tubes' in the

US). However, such installations were unduly large, using up prodigious amounts of electrical energy and generating a lot of waste heat. And they didn't have much memory by today's standards – around 40 kilobytes was typical. The invention of the transistor in 1959, enabled much smaller computers to be built, which were cheaper, used much less power and could have much more memory. And so, by the late 1970s, desktop 'micro-computers' became available commercially for businesses, schools – and, indeed, for the home user. Many of these used a simple programming language called BASIC (Beginner's All-purpose Symbolic Instruction Code). Other programming languages including COBOL and FORTRAN were also available for business and scientific users, and the like. A simple example of a BASIC program is the following:

```
10 LET Z=0
20 FOR I=1 TO 10
30 INPUT X
40 LET Z=Z+X
50 NEXT I
60 LET Z=Z/10
70 PRINT "AVERAGE = ";Z
80 END
```

This program allows the user to input ten numbers, calculates their average and then displays the result on a screen. (If a printed copy of the result is required, then the command LPRINT is used instead of PRINT.)

Using a programming language such as BASIC, it is possible to build up a variety of quite complex programs, including some that appear to converse with the user. While it superficially looks like intelligent behaviour on the part of the computer, this is not actually the case. The computer is simply following a strict algorithmic procedure which has already been programmed into it. The 'intelligence' at work here is that of the (human) programmer and not of the machine itself.

Modern computers are supplied not with a programming language but with 'packages' – bundles of pre-installed programs designed to perform specific functions. (Programming languages can, nevertheless, still be purchased and installed as an additional item.) The most widely used packages include word-processing, spreadsheets, databases, computer graphics and games packages. Word-processing packages now are so sophisticated that they will correct faulty spelling and grammar, and usually also provide a comprehensive thesaurus. And the best computer chess-playing programs are now so good that they are capable of beating the best grand masters. Again, these examples look like intelligent behaviour on the part of the computer, but they are not. As always, it is the programmer who must take the credit.

Artificial Intelligence

Computer software engineers have, in recent years, developed systems whereby computers can, at least to some extent, self-program – effectively learning from experience. This is known as *heuristic* programming, and is part of an ongoing project to determine whether it is possible to build a truly 'conscious' machine. What this entails is that the computer is 'taught' (for example) how to read a handwritten script by presenting it with various examples, and then allowing it to 'read' other scripts in which the legibility is poorer.

Heuristic programming shows such great potential that it will, in years to come, *appear* that we have succeeded in building a 'conscious' robot or computer. But, as always, we should be wary of this. We should reflect on those mental activities which we manage with ease, but which computers still cannot do at all. Computers don't dream, fantasize or demonstrate a sense of humour. Indeed, one of the biggest challenges we could throw at any kind of artificial intelligence is the ability to interpret *cartoons* – especially political cartoons. In this medium, the facial characteristics of politicians (and others) are so wildly exaggerated that they are barely recognizable – the cartoons of Gerald Scarfe being a notable example. We *do* instantly recognize the people depicted in the cartoons, but machines cannot do this.

The interpretation of political cartoons entails more than just recognizing faces, however. The cartoons are highly nuanced in their subject matter, and it takes an appreciation of both the current political situation and other items of interest in the news, as well as the ability to recognize grossly distorted faces, to interpret any political cartoon. I may be wrong, but I do not foresee any computer ever being able to accomplish this.

While political cartoons present a major – probably insurmountable – challenge to computer intelligence, this is maybe not the ultimate challenge. In my own mental reflections I sometimes wonder *why* I am who I am. *Why* am I a human and not an animal? *Why*, out of billions and billions of people, am I always aware of being Anthony Burns, and never anyone else? No computer could ever ask such questions of itself, let alone answer them.

In brain terms, computers are able to perform *some* of the functions of the left cerebral hemisphere – often more successfully than we can. But they operate on a radically different physical principle.

Human experience – and presumably animal experience also – is dominated by *qualia* (pronounced 'kwahl-ya') which are the *subjective* experiences resulting from brain activity. A physicist can, for example, measure the wavelength of red light, and also determine that it a vibration of an electromagnetic field. But the actual *experience* of redness is something that cannot be expressed in physical terms. It is something purely subjective – and it is something that computers can never 'know' about.

Referring back, once more, to Professor Lorber's mathematics student who had no brain, this student was effectively able to think with no 'hardware' at all. But a computer without hardware would not even exist, let alone demonstrate any kind of 'intelligence'.

8: Rule by Mathematics

The physical sciences are so dominated by mathematics that it almost seems that they are themselves just a branch of mathematics. Mathematics is certainly a useful tool, indispensable in fact, for both the physical scientist and the engineer. Mathematics differs from the other sciences, however, because of its abstract nature. Its laws remain valid, even when they have no physical expression or conceivable application in the physical world.

An example of this is in the realm of very large numbers. I can, for example, count five digits (four fingers and a thumb) on my hand. I can readily comprehend what a set of five objects looks like. If, however, I were to count up all the elementary particles (quarks, electrons, etc.) in the whole universe and then place that number of zeroes after the five, I would obtain a number that is so ridiculously large that it couldn't possibly represent anything in the real world. *But, in mathematical terms, this large number is just as valid a number as five is.* We could say, then, that five *manifests*, since we can appreciate what five objects look like; but the very large number does not manifest. Mathematics is thus a valid science, even in the abstract.

Mathematics is also unique among the sciences in that its laws do not change over time. This is not necessarily the case with the physical sciences, as there is some suggestion that physical constants such as the speed of light may, over many centuries, slowly change – ultimately leading to changes in the laws of physics themselves. This is not so with mathematics.

Numbers and Computation
For nearly all of us, our first introduction to mathematics was through the numbers. First, we learnt to count, then we learnt to add, subtract, multiply and divide, using those numbers. Later

still, many of us learnt more advanced computational methods, including the use of logarithms and the calculation of square roots. Since we have five digits on each hand (ten in all) and counting on one's fingers is a useful method of tallying, we have adopted a system of reckoning in tens – the decimal system. We do not have to use a base of ten, however. The ancient Sumerians reckoned to a base of 60, and computers utilize a base of two. This latter is for practical reasons since a computer is essentially a bank of switches, each of which may be 'on' (one) or 'off' (zero). Only these two digits are used, but this has the result that even relatively small numbers look unduly long when printed out. The number 64, for example is rendered in binary as 1000000, requiring seven digits instead of the usual two.

There are also systems of reckoning known as *modulo* arithmetic whereby the addition of two positive numbers may produce a *smaller* number as the result. This is most easily seen on a conventional clock face (modulo 12). When we add three hours to eleven o'clock, for example, the result is *two*, not fourteen.

The laws governing arithmetic operations are summarized as *algebra*, which is not really a separate subject from computation except that letters are substituted for unknown quantities. Algebra is thus a generalization of the laws of arithmetic. Conversely, arithmetic could be described as 'applied algebra'. Algebra is mostly concerned with either solving equations to find unknown quantities or else proving that particular algebraic expressions are equivalent to each other.

'Special' Numbers

Certain of the numbers have such unusual properties that they stand out from the rest, and it is worthwhile to take a look at some of these.

The Square Root of 2 ($\sqrt{2}$) is interesting in that it cannot be expressed as a ratio between two integers or as a 'tidy' decimal.

The Greek philosophers spent many hours puzzling over this. Written in decimal form, $\sqrt{2}$ appears as 1.41414 ... ad infinitum. Its *precise* value can never be represented using decimal notation.

Pi *(π)* is the ratio between the circumference and diameter of a circle (drawn on a flat plane). It too is an infinitely long decimal, but in this case there are *no* repeating sequences of digits. Its decimal value is approximately 3.14159265358 ... , usually written as 3.142 or 3.1416. School pupils are often taught to use the approximation 22/7.

The Exponential Coefficient (e) Like pi, the exponential coefficient is an infinitely long, non-repeating decimal, having an approximate value of 2.71812... Again it is a number that occurs in nature – hence its 'special' status – and is the number associated with *exponential growth*.

The 'Golden Ratio', usually represented by the Greek Letter Φ (phi) is yet another endless non-repeating decimal, having the value: 1.618033988749 ... (being equal to $(1 + \sqrt{5})/2$. It has remarkable properties in that:

$$1/\Phi = \Phi - 1$$
$$\text{and } \Phi^2 = \Phi + 1$$

(Any reader with a calculator to hand can easily check these results.) Closely linked to the Golden Ratio is the *Fibonacci series*, a series of numbers in which each number is the sum of the previous two. It runs thus:

0 1 1 2 3 5 8 13 21 34 55 89 ...

When the ratios between successive pairs of numbers in this series are compared, it is found that these converge toward the Golden Ratio.

The Fibonacci numbers occur in nature in numerous, often unexpected, ways. The numbers of leaves on a plant stem and the number of stamens or petals on a flower are nearly always numbers in the Fibonacci series. Starfish and sea urchins always have a five-fold radial symmetry, five being a Fibonacci number. Fibonacci numbers are present also in musical scales, the penta-tonic scale (5 notes) combining with the octave (8 notes) to produce a 'chromatic' scale of 13 notes.

Zero and Infinity When we divide a finite number by zero we get infinity. But infinity is not a number in the normal sense. It does not make sense to try to add or subtract using infinity. Infinity minus one is still infinity. Also, there is no 'largest' finite number, since no matter how large the number we are thinking of, we can always add one to that number. It is thus impossible to count all the way up to infinity.

Infinity also has the strange property in that we can subtract infinity from itself and still be left with infinity. If space is infinite in all three dimensions and we cut a thin slice out of it, the volume of the slice will be infinity – as will be the volume that is left.

Counting and Measuring

There are two ways in which numbers may be used in compu-tation, and there is an important difference between the two. These are counting and measuring. If we have (say) eight jelly beans, there can be no doubt that there are eight. Any other number would be incorrect. If, however, I were to express the length of a table, I would have to specify what *units* I was using. A measurement using inches will give a different numerical result from one using centimetres, even though the length is the same. If we were to contrive different systems of units, then *any* number could represent an accurate measurement of any given length.

Computation in physics mostly involves measurements and calculations of the latter type; it is rare in physics for readings to be taken merely by counting objects. There are, however instances in which physical quantities can be combined (through multiplying and dividing) to give *dimensionless* quantities – yielding the same number regardless of what units of measurement are used. An example of this is the *fine structure constant*, used in spectroscopy, which has a value tantalizingly close to 1/137.

Dimensional Analysis

The calculations we perform in physics are generally concerned with physical *measurements* which have been made. These include mass, length, time, electric charge and various quantities derived by multiplying, dividing and otherwise combining these 'basic' units. It is an important principle in any mathematical equation (not just in physics) that the units on either side of the equation are always the same. We cannot, for example, say that x kilograms equals y centimetres – such an 'equation' simply would not make sense. The purpose of dimensional analysis is principally to establish the units of any quantities derived from actual physical measurements and also to check that the equation makes sense mathematically.

The basic physical units normally used in dimensional analysis are mass (M), length (L), time (T) and electric charge (Q). Most other physical units are derivations of these four so that, for example, velocity is length (or distance) divided by time (L/T).

We do not necessarily have to use these four as the basic units, however. Quantities such as energy, momentum and angular momentum are, in fact, more easily expressed in terms of *force*, length and time. Thus energy is expressed as force times distance (FL), momentum as force times time (FT) and angular momentum as the product of all three (FLT).

The discovery of the Planck length and Planck time (which we saw in Chapter 5) is attributable to performing dimensional analysis on various mathematical combinations of the natural physical constants, notably (in this case) Newton's gravitational constant (G), Planck's constant (h) and the speed of light (c). Thus $\sqrt{(Gh/c^3)}$ has units of length and $\sqrt{(Gh/c^5)}$ has units of time. As we have already seen, these quantities are much too small to be observed or measured directly; they can only be inferred from dimensional analysis

Geometry

The study of geometry is a separate branch of mathematics, largely independent of algebra and computation, and is concerned with shapes and configurations occurring in space. At first sight, much of what we encounter in geometry may seem trivial. Euclid declared that space was 'flat' in that the shortest distance between any two points always had to be a straight line. Also, in Euclidian space, the circumference of a circle is given as $2\pi r$ and its area is given as πr^2 (r being the radius of the circle) – and the angles of a triangle drawn in Euclidian space always add up to 180 degrees (two right angles). Descartes expanded on Euclid's idea, proposing that the position of any point in space could be defined using three numbers, namely, distance to the right (x), distance forward (y) and distance upward (z). This is known as the system of *Cartesian co-ordinates.*

There are alternatives to the Cartesian system, however, notably the system of *polar co-ordinates.* This may involve measuring the distance from a central point and a pair of angles to determine the position of the point in question (spherical co-ordinates) or, alternatively, the distance from a central axis, an angle and the distance *along* that axis (cylindrical co-ordinates).

Figures drawn on the surface of a sphere do not conform to the Euclidian model: instead, the shortest distance between two points on its surface is *not* a straight line but an arc-length of the *great circle* passing through both of those points. Such a line is known as a *geodesic.* The geometries of the circle and the triangle also change when these are drawn on the surface of a sphere.

Since the nineteenth century, other alternatives to the Euclidian model have been developed, notably by the German mathematicians David Hilbert and Bernhard Riemann. Modern physicists (including Einstein) have seriously considered whether the universe might conform to one of these alternative geometries, rather than the Euclidian model.

Graphs

In the most general sense, graphs are a geometric representation of algebraic equations or relations. Instead of solving an equation directly, we may plot the corresponding 'y' values for a given set of 'x' values, and then join up the points thus plotted to form a continuous curve. Graphs are widely used to indicate how different quantities change over a period of time, and are especially useful in both weather forecasting and economic forecasting.

Geometric problems may also be converted into algebraic ones by plotting geometric shapes on a graph and then setting up algebraic equations, using the measurements obtained from the graph. This is the converse of solving equations using a graph, and is known as *co-ordinate geometry.*

Probability and Statistics

We have already seen some examples of statistics at work in Chapter 4, but the range of possible applications is much broader than this. Computing averages and deviations from these average values is probably the best known use of statistics, but the subject also includes the testing of hypotheses, and of finding the 'best' line that will fit a set of scattered points on a graph.

Probability is the study of how likely it is that a particular event will occur. For example, the probability of landing a '6' when throwing a die is one in six, since the die has six faces.

Calculus

The third main branch of mathematics, beside algebra and geometry, is calculus. This is the study of *rates of change*. As an example, velocity is the rate of change of linear displacement (distance travelled), and acceleration is the rate of change of velocity. Sir Isaac Newton first developed the methods of calculus to facilitate the computation of planetary orbits. Leibnitz also developed calculus (using different notation) independently of Newton, and there was much rivalry between the two men over which of them came up with the idea first.

The process of calculating a rate of change is called *differentiation*, the rate of change itself being called the *differential*. More advanced methods in calculus involve *differential equations* in which the differentials themselves are treated like the unknown quantities in algebra. The solution to a differential equation is therefore not a numerical value (or set of values) but another equation, one in which there are no differentials.

The reverse process of differentiation is called *integration*.

Iteration

At times it is difficult to perform a calculation and obtain a numerical result using the 'normal' methods of calculation – a situation that often occurs in calculus problems. However, it is often possible to find the required result by performing a simple calculation repeatedly, feeding the results back into the calculation each time. This method is known as *iteration*. We may use it, for example, to find a square root. Let us suppose we wish to find the square root of 39. We can apply the method as follows:

Start with 39
Divide by (say) 6:
$39 = 6 \times 6.5$ (1st iteration)
We now know that the square root lies somewhere between 6 and 6.5

Divide by a number between 6 and 6.5, (say) 6.2
39 = 6.2 x 6.29 (2nd iteration)
Divide by (say) 6.25:
39 = 6.25 x 6.24 (3rd iteration)
Divide by 6.245:
39 = 6.245 x 6.245 (4th iteration)
Thus √39 = 6.245 (accurate to 3 decimal places)

After only four iterations, we have already established the square root of 39 to no less than three decimal places. We could, of course, perform further iterations to obtain more decimal places if we wished, but this example shows the simplicity of the method.

Fractals

An interesting corollary of the iterative process is the development of fractals. These are curves that display a regular pattern which repeats on every scale – with the result that when we look at that pattern, we don't know on what scale we are looking at it. Coastlines are good examples of fractals: they show more and more complexity when mapped on a larger and larger scale. One of the best known examples of a fractal created mathematically is the *Koch snowflake* which is built up, in the first instance, from an equilateral triangle. (See Figure 10.)

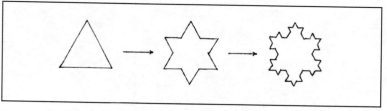

Fig. 10: Evolution of a Fractal: the Koch 'Snowflake'

The rule applied here (and iterated) is that we divide each side of the figure into three equal sections and then fit another equilateral triangle over the middle section. Each time the iteration is done, the total length of the boundary of the figure is increased by a factor of 4/3. This means that, after an infinite number of iterations, (when we have a true 'fractal') we have an infinitely long boundary enclosing an area that is still finite in size. The boundary has a further extraordinary property: in calculus terms, it is differentiable *nowhere* – even though it is continuous everywhere. (In practice, this means that the boundary has no straight sections *anywhere*, however small the scale.)

Chaos Theory (The Butterfly Effect)

It used to be thought that very small discrepancies in the starting conditions for any process would make little difference to the final outcome. We now know that this is not the case – weather forecasting being a notorious example. Scientists have suggested that the tiny air current produced by a flapping butterfly wing can, over a matter of weeks, escalate into a hurricane – usually in another part of the world. (Hence the name *the Butterfly Effect*)

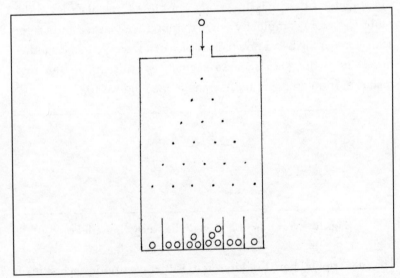

Fig. 11: The Pinboard Experiment

The pinboard experiment (Fig. 11) demonstrates this. As each ball is dropped in at the top and hits the first pin, it may bounce either right or left. It is the same for every subsequent pin, so that the ball may finally land in any of the slots at the bottom of the apparatus. It is virtually impossible for the experimenter to predict where any ball will land, or to aim for any particular slot.

Further examples of chaotic behaviour can be observed in the swing of a jointed pendulum and in the behaviour of magnetic compasses when they are stacked on top of one another.

Cellular Automata

In 1967, H A Conway reported on a mathematical 'game' which he had developed. This involved using a large grid of squares – which he referred to as 'cells' – each of which was designated as either 'live' or 'dead'. He then applied a simple iterative rule and observed how the shapes defined by the 'live' cells would evolve. The rule was: a 'live' cell would survive into the next generation if it was adjacent (orthogonally or diagonally) to either two or three other 'live' cells; otherwise it would die. Also, a 'dead' cell would become 'live' in the next generation if it was adjacent to exactly three other cells which were already 'live'. There were no other rules. Because of the size and complexity of the figures that could evolve, it was almost always necessary to run the game on a computer.

Figure 12 shows how certain simple shapes would evolve when the rule was applied, each iteration resulting in the next 'generation'. One of the more complex shapes (not shown) was a 'glider gun' which fired more and more 'gliders' (Fig. 12d) which, many thought, resembled the life process itself in that these figures were self-reproducing. The process was therefore dubbed the *Game of Life*. (The experimenters even felt guilty about turning the machine off at the end of the day, as they felt that they were killing off 'living' things.)

In the examples shown here, the Blinker (Fig.12a) oscillates

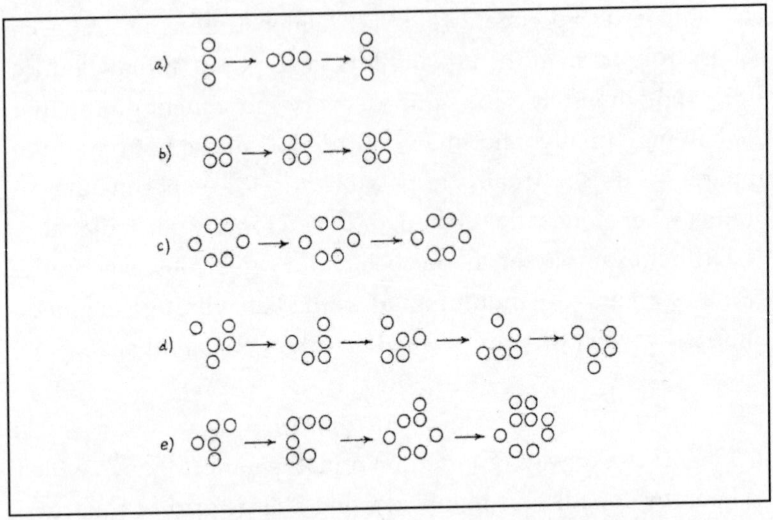

Fig. 12: Conway's 'Game of Life' – Some Examples: a) Blinker; b) Block; c) Beehive; d) Glider; e) r-pentomino

between two states, the Block (Fig.12b) and the Beehive (Fig.12c) are both stable and the Glider regains its original shape (having drifted one square diagonally) after every fourth iteration. The r-pentomino (Fig.12e) has a very long history, developing into a large and complex array of evolving and interacting shapes before it finally 'settles down' – after more than a thousand iterations.

Other cellular automata have been developed in addition to Conway's game, including three-dimensional ones and some using a hexagonal array instead of the square grid used here. For many years cellular automata were thought to be just an amusing game. However, at least one physicist has suggested that this type of mathematical modelling may hold an important clue regarding the nature of elementary particles.

The remarkable thing about the whole of mathematics, as we saw earlier, is that its laws are valid without necessarily having any external application. We saw that there are numbers which are so large that they could never have any conceivable application or manifestation in the real world. And the laws of mathematics can never change. Even in the absence of any kind of physical universe, the laws of mathematics will still hold. Even Conway's rules for the *Game of Life* should, in theory, be no exception to this.

Does mathematics help at all in our understanding of the strange events we encountered in Chapter 1? Not necessarily. But mathematics is the foundation of the physical sciences and so cannot be ignored. From our point of view, the underlying *philosophy* of mathematics is probably more relevant than the actual computational techniques used. We must bear in mind, though, that not everything that happens in the real world can *readily* be described using mathematics. If I listen to a Beethoven symphony and feel inspired to write a symphony of my own, there is no obvious way in which this could be predicted or described using mathematics. However, music has a mathematical logic of its own – as does the physical process of writing it down. Even if its influence is only a subtle one, we may safely say that mathematical laws underlie all of physical manifestation.

9: Science at the Crossroads

Contemporary scientific research has reached a point at which it could *possibly* start to explain at least some of the bizarre phenomena catalogued in Chapter 1. But as yet it hasn't done so. Scientists are exceptionally cautious and sceptical in how they pursue their work, and will not base their theories merely on anecdotal evidence, no matter how well authenticated this might be. As we have seen, however, modern science itself paints a picture of the world which itself seems to defy all credibility. The special theory of relativity indicates a possible 'block universe' in which the future is predetermined and events which are simultaneous for one observer aren't necessarily simultaneous for anyone else. And the world of quantum mechanics is one in which every elementary 'particle' is also a wave, can be in several different places at once and can also interact with particles at the other end of the universe by the phenomenon of *entanglement*. Brain science has come a long way toward explaining how the brain 'works', but still cannot explain our own subjective experience of 'conscious awareness'. And Professor Lorber's discovery of a university student without any sign of a physical brain defies explanation. Brain science, to use an analogy, tells us how the car works, but says nothing about the driver. We still do not know for certain how brains – or, indeed, the life process itself – first came into existence. Notwithstanding the great strides that science has made during the last century and a half, there are still huge gaps in our knowledge.

According to the laws of physics, as we currently understand them, we ought not to be here at all. We are an impossibility. And yet here we are, able to discuss and philosophize about these things. All physics is able to offer in the way of an explanation is the second law of thermodynamics – a state of affairs in which, figuratively speaking, the dominoes are eternally being shuffled and re-shuffled. We can never have a completed game of dominoes if the shuffling never stops. And yet some of the materials created billions of years ago (and supposedly obeying the second law of thermodynamics) have ended up as cars, aeroplanes, computers, television sets – and us. Something else is clearly going on besides the second law of thermodynamics.

The 'Peer Review' Process

It is useful at this point to examine how research scientists actually go about their work. They perform experiments, often to test hypotheses, but sometimes just to see what might happen. And then they publish the results. Before the results are published, however, these are first reviewed by other scientists. This is the process known as *peer review.* For the most part, peer review works very well. If we didn't have it, we would have to invent it. It prevents individual scientists (and research teams) from 'going off the rails' by promoting anything too outlandish. The process is not unlike piloting a big ship in that it prevents the ship from bumping against the rocks. *But can it turn the ship around if it has gone down a blind alleyway?* Not necessarily.

Sometimes it takes a 'maverick' scientist – someone from outside the mainstream scientific community – to provide the insight that is needed before a breakthrough can be made. Often they are loners who have spent many years working on pet projects of their own. Often they get things wrong, and are ridiculed for it. But sometimes – just occasionally – they strike it lucky. Several of the great names from the past were mavericks in their own day, and it may be instructive to see who some of these were.

Maverick Scientists

I could start by mentioning some of the ancient Greek philosophers (Socrates, Plato, Aristotle), but in their day, science as we know it now hadn't yet begun. These people were philosophers, rather than scientists. They formulated their theories but, to the best of our knowledge, hardly did any experiments at all.

Probably the earliest people we could properly class as scientists (and mavericks in their day) were *Copernicus* and *Galileo*, both renowned for their pioneering work on the solar system. Copernicus, probably quite wisely, withheld his research results until he was on his deathbed. Galileo subsequently had to face the flak from the Roman Catholic Church, ostensibly for pointing a telescope at Jupiter and its satellites, and daring to say that the earth was not the centre of the universe. Sir Isaac Newton later gave substance to the Copernican model when he formulated his theory of gravitation. But he too was an odd character who could definitely (in his own way) be classed as a maverick.

Charles Darwin, though not necessarily an 'odd' personality, clearly qualifies as a maverick. His suggestion that the human species was descended from apes or monkeys triggered a furore of epic proportions, especially among orthodox religious people who believed the Book of Genesis. Even today, his ideas are controversial in some quarters.

Another maverick from more recent times – and still a largely unsung hero – was *Nikola Tesla*. Unusually for a scientist, he was also psychically sensitive (he saw a deathbed vision of his mother when she died) and his pioneering work on electricity and magnetism was decades ahead of his own time. He is also said to have received an extraordinary insight into the nature of electricity and magnetism on one occasion when he gazed into a sunset. Many of his inventions subsequently were either suppressed (mainly for commercial reasons) or taken up by other inventors, notably Edison and Marconi. In any case, we can thank Tesla for the invention of alternating current for the public electricity supply.

Both *Albert Einstein* and (to some extent) *Max Planck* may be seen as mavericks because of the extraordinary nature of their theories, although Planck himself was ultra-conservative in outlook, and didn't personally like the theory he was proposing.

A more recent maverick, still controversial in scientific circles, was *Eric Laithwaite* who, like Tesla, worked on electricity and magnetism. He also worked on gyroscopes, seeing a possible connection with electrical phenomena. He fell out of favour with the scientific establishment when he suggested that gyroscopes could possibly function as an anti-gravity device – still a doubtful proposition. The idea of a link between gyroscopes and electrical phenomena is interesting, however, and merits further investigation.

There are others from more recent times who are currently seen as mavericks and not taken seriously by the scientific establishment. I name Rupert Sheldrake and Ivan T Sanderson as two of these. Whether any of them ever become accepted as 'mainstream' scientists, only time will tell.

Whither Science?

As always, scientific research is a work in progress. Experimental work must continue, since it is only from actual experimental results that any theories proposed can be either confirmed or refuted. (This can often, especially these days, require the expenditure of large sums of money.) Professional scientists nowadays are both fortunate and unfortunate. They are fortunate in that they are being paid for their work – but they are unfortunate in that whoever pays the piper calls the tune. Often they are engaged specifically to find scientific confirmation of ideas already put forward by vested interests (whether business or government) – and can all too often find themselves in trouble if their conclusions differ from what was 'expected' of them. Some are lucky enough to be engaged in 'blue sky' research (in which they are free to investigate whatever interests them), but many are not.

The scientific community, for all its pioneering work, is remarkably conservative in its underlying philosophy. Most scientists are cautious in their acceptance of new ideas, and wary of anything that seems too outlandish. There is nothing wrong with this. It is generally the best approach to take. However, as any scientist will tell us, the importance of accurate observation can never be over-emphasized. And accurate observation must be followed up by keeping accurate records. Photography and other means of physical recording provide the best records of all.

Overall, by following these methods, scientists do a good job. But they should nevertheless remain open to the insights that an occasional 'maverick' scientist might bring.

The state of play is such that science, especially over the last century and a half, has made predictions which are truly bizarre in their own right, but which have repeatedly been confirmed by experiment. Much of what has been found appears contradictory or counter-intuitive. Both relativity and quantum theory have excelled as much in their weirdness as in their ability to explain the true nature of the world in which we live.

The main discoveries that have been made by scientists over the past two centuries may be summarized as follows:

- Electrical and magnetic phenomena are closely linked and are essentially different aspects of the same thing.
- Light and similar radiations (radio waves, X-rays, etc.) are the result of an oscillating electric/magnetic field.
- Light is quantized, each photon having an energy proportional to its rate of vibration.
- Atoms are assemblies (resembling miniature solar systems) of much smaller particles, known as 'elementary' particles.
- Elementary particles are classified by a system known as the Standard Model.
- Elementary particles sometimes behave as waves, rather than particles.
- A single elementary particle may be in several places at

once.

- The speed of light is the same for all observers, no matter how they are moving in space.
- The mass of an object depends on how fast it is moving through space.
- The rate of flow of time can be variable.
- Observers can disagree on which events are simultaneous.
- 'Empty' space is filled with pairs of particles which continuously generate and annihilate (known as *virtual particles*).
- 'Empty' space exerts a slight pressure on objects contained within it (the Casimir effect).
- 'Empty' space gets pulled around a rotating object (frame dragging);
- Most of the mass of the universe is unaccounted for by the presence of matter and is (provisionally) being attributed to 'dark matter'.
- Light from distant parts of the universe is red-shifted, suggesting that the universe is expanding.
- Large, very dense concentrations of matter are known as black holes. Nothing can escape from a black hole – even light. *However*, the continued generation and annihilation of virtual particles in the space surrounding a black hole causes some particles to 'leak' from the black hole (known as *Hawking radiation*, after Stephen Hawking who first suggested it).

Attempts to reconcile quantum theory with relativity and gravitation have not, so far, been very successful. This is still an area of ongoing research. The main theories put forward to try to resolve this dilemma have, so far, been string theory (of which there are five versions), M-theory and loop quantum gravity (LQG). The latter predicts that space and time are themselves both quantized.

As the body of confirmed scientific knowledge grows, this

seems to open up more and more unanswered questions. We know how entities such as mass and electric charge behave – but we still don't know what they really *are*. We don't know what time is, except that we measure it with a clock. And, most importantly, we don't know what the *observer* is. We know that the 'observer' is us, and brain science has given us some clues. But we don't know the true nature of our own 'conscious awareness' and what produces it, or of how we came to be here in the first place.

At the risk of becoming dubbed a 'fringe scientist' myself, I offer a few *suggestions* on new lines of enquiry which future generations of scientists may care to explore. These are *not* theories as such, but hints at further questions that scientists might ask. Any of these ideas may be confirmed or refuted by future experimental results.

- Mass may be an inherent property of space (or spacetime) itself. If so, it would explain why 'dark matter' has never been observed.
- The wave/particle dilemma for elementary particles may be better understood if we imagine them as knots and ripples in the fabric of spacetime itself.
- If this is so, then there may have to be a *second* space or spacetime against which the distortions of the first can be compared.
- There may not have been a Big Bang. The universe may expand and contract periodically.
- Time may be cyclic, with the history of the universe endlessly repeating.
- There may be even more dimensions than the eleven proposed by LQG. These may be organized into nested 'spaces' of one, three, seven and fifteen dimensions respectively.
- The extra dimensions are said by physicists to be 'rolled up

very small'. There may be an alternative to this: dimensions that 'ride on the backs' of others. A simple example would be time which, for a moving object, could be said to be 'riding on the back' of the spatial dimension along which that object is moving.

- We think that 'reality' is an all-or-none affair. But there may, in fact, be different levels or grades of reality.
- There may be only one observer in the whole universe.

I wish my scientific colleagues the best of luck if they care to follow up on any of these suggestions. We clearly don't know all of the laws of physics; if we did, then most scientists would be out of a job. There would be nothing left for them to research. If we take the surface of the earth as representing all of the laws of physics, both known and unknown, then what we already know is probably equivalent to a country the size of Luxembourg. Scientists may rest assured that they will have plenty of work for many years to come.

The remaining big gap in our scientific knowledge is that we don't know what the *observer* is. We know that it's us – but that's about all. It is possible that science will *never* produce an answer to this fundamental question. And if science cannot find the answer then, perhaps, we ought to turn to philosophy.

III : The Philosophy

10: Philosophy and Science

What is philosophy, and how does it differ from science? Both are part of a general quest for the truth and, indeed, the earliest 'scientists' (if we can call them that) were the ancient Greek philosophers. At that time, science was not seen as a distinct subject from philosophy, as it is today, and philosophers pondered over questions in both science and mathematics, as well as in what we would now call 'philosophy'. In this respect, Pythagoras and Euclid are among the early pioneers in mathematical discovery. In science, however, not very much real progress was made, apart from Aristotle's classification of living things and Archimedes' discovery of the principle of flotation, which (legend says) came to him while he was having a bath. The Greek philosophers, notably Democritus and Leucippus, correctly guessed that matter was made up of atoms, as opposed to being smooth and continuous; but they never did any experiments to confirm their theories. Had they thought of it, they might have realized that when an oil drop spreads into a thin film on water, it only spreads so far and then stops. At this point the oil film is only one atom (or molecule) thick – evidence of the particulate nature of matter. Also, in the light of modern science, they were wrong in suggesting that all matter was made from just four elements – fire, earth, air and water.

One of the most influential philosophers of the last few centuries has been René Descartes. We have already encountered the system of mathematical co-ordinates which he devised (the Cartesian system). What is less well known is that he asked of himself a number of fundamental questions concerning his own (and our) existence. His line of reasoning ran thus:

I can doubt that the world exists.
I can even doubt that my own body exists.

But I cannot doubt that *I* exist.

Descartes thus came to the conclusion that the soul or spirit was an entity distinct from the physical body. Philosophers refer to this view as *dualism*.

Philosophy has also, traditionally, been concerned with matters of morality and of social and political organization. The economist Adam Smith, along with other names such as Jeremy Bentham, John Stuart Mill and even Karl Marx clearly qualify as philosophers on this count. Political philosophy is of little relevance to our own line of enquiry, however.

Since the early part of the twentieth century, philosophy has been largely concerned with an analysis of *language*. Bertrand Russell and Alfred North Whitehead were among the pioneers in this respect. Modern philosophers dissect the language to try to establish what every statement 'really' means. They pose questions such as:

How old is 'old'?
Where does your lap go when you stand up?
Where is the National Anthem when it isn't being sung?
If a woman has lost her good looks, where did she lose them?
Did she leave them behind in the coffee shop?

Questions such as these are, of course, unanswerable and almost have the quality of Buddhist koans (an example of which is *the sound of one hand clapping*). Examination of such questions may reveal a lot about the language itself, but it tells us nothing about the world in which we live.

Our principal 'tools' for studying and analyzing the world are:

Numbers
Images – usually conveyed as maps, photographs or

diagrams

Words and sentences

All of these are indispensable, both for studying the world and for communicating our perceptions and ideas to others. Numbers (and other mathematical concepts) are, as we have seen, fundamental properties of the universe itself, and follow laws that would hold even in the absence of a physical universe. Maps and diagrams, if well drawn and presented can likewise convey vast amounts of valuable information – although it must never be forgotten (as Escher demonstrated) that it is possible to draw pictures of 'impossible' objects, as shown in Figure 13. Language (notably the English language, because of its large vocabulary) is the most flexible tool of all – but it has its limitations. It is useful at this point to take a brief look at the underlying nature of language and its possible origins.

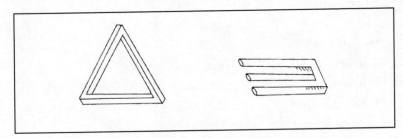

Fig. 13: Escher's 'Impossible' Pictures – Two Classic Examples

Language and Synaesthesia

Some of us (myself included) have a peculiar habit of associating numbers, days of the week, months and letters of the alphabet with particular colours, aromas and the like. (The composer Jean Sibelius is known to have associated musical keys with colours.) This phenomenon is known to psychologists as *synaesthesia*. Other forms of synaesthesia include associating smells and tastes with other sensory impressions, assigning genders to inanimate objects, and arranging numbers, dates and letters of the alphabet into elaborate spatial patterns. Psychologists have, in the past, speculated that the colour associations are acquired by children playing with toy bricks bearing coloured letters and numbers. More recent research on the subject, however, has indicated that this is not generally the case.

What is particularly interesting about synaesthesia is that the centres in the brain responsible for such associations are, in many cases, physically very close to the language areas. This, it would appear, could shed light on the very origin of language itself. It may, ultimately, turn out that language itself is simply a very elaborate form of synaesthesia that everyone possesses. (This could explain why many of the world's languages assign arbitrary genders to inanimate objects and ideas.) Extending this idea, the ability to read and write must confer an extraordinary three-way synaesthesia – to say nothing about being multi-lingual! When we consider the matter, we have to admit that nearly all the words of any language are no more than arbitrary labels which bear no relation to the objects or ideas which they are meant to represent. The first chapter of the *Tao te Ching* sums it up beautifully:

> *The name that can be named is not the eternal name.*
> *The way that can be spoken of is not the eternal way.*

This says it all. We use the language as best we can to put our ideas across. We also, quite often, use it for processing ideas. We should remember, however, that there are ideas and concepts that are beyond the reach of any language. (The 'hidden compass' phenomenon discussed in Chapter 2 could be an example of this – which would explain why there has been so little discussion about it.)

To obtain a true picture of how the universe 'really' is, we really need to put language aside for a while, and give our imagination free rein. Einstein was very good at this. He imagined what it must be like to ride on a beam of light. He visualized himself receding backwards at the speed of light from the famous *Zytglogge* clock in Berne, where he lived, and realized that in this situation he would see the clock hands as stationary – and frozen in time. He didn't need any language to visualize this.

We are all at liberty to flex our imagination just as much as Einstein did. However, we need to be careful about what we imagine. I can imagine all sorts of impossible things. For example, I can imagine the moon falling out of the sky and landing on someone's head. I can imagine railway trains being powered by mice in treadmills. I can imagine heavy loads being lifted up by no force other than pure levitation. I can imagine (and have observed) physical objects being de-materialized and teleported. And, as we saw earlier, I can imagine many of the strange things that we would observe if time were to run backwards. It is all too easy to get carried away by flights of fancy. But, as we have seen, the universe is a bizarre place where things don't always go to plan, anyway. And yet – somewhere – amidst all the chaos – ought to be the key to reality itself.

What is Reality?

We like to think that we live in a world that is stable, dependable and predictable. And, happily for us, it does seem to behave this way for most of the time. Modern science, however, has indicated that beyond the veneer of everyday life is a world that is almost impossible to believe or imagine. Arthur C Clarke once said that the world was even stranger than we could ever imagine it to be. The bizarre events we saw in Chapter 1 are evidence of this. So what do we actually mean when we talk of 'reality'?

We habitually think of reality as an all-or-none affair: either something is real, or it is not. The discoveries of relativity and quantum physics have already cast doubt on this, however.

Imagine the following scenario: four people are sitting around a table on which there may – or may not – be a candlestick. If all four people see a candlestick on the table, we would normally conclude that the candlestick is *real*. The candlestick has an objective existence. Conversely, if none of the people sees a candlestick, then the logical conclusion is that there is no candlestick on the table. Any candlestick there is *not real.* However, there are other possibilities. If one person sees a candlestick but the other three don't, we would normally conclude that there is no candlestick there, and that the person who sees one is hallucinating. And if three people see a candlestick but one doesn't, we would normally infer that there *is* a candlestick present, and that the person who fails to see it is either asleep or not paying attention. There is yet a fifth possibility – one which we would normally dismiss out of hand – but which *can* sometimes happen. If *two* people see a candlestick on the table, and the other two don't, *is the candlestick real?* Science cannot answer this question. Indeed, there is no ready answer. However, the episodes reported from Boscastle (Chapter 1, Case 3) and Montélimar (Case 4) are evidence that situations of this nature *do* sometimes arise.

Modern physics has already suggested that every observer has his or her own reality. We have seen this in the special theory of relativity, and there are hints also in quantum physics. The 'hidden compass' phenomenon is a further indication that not everyone sees the world in exactly the same way. It may be that, rather than treating 'reality' as an all-or-none affair, we may have to consider different grades or levels of reality. We could, if mathematically inclined, assign to everything a numerical *coefficient of reality*, ranging from zero to one hundred percent. Thus when two people see the candlestick on the table, and the other two don't, we might legitimately say that the candlestick is 'fifty percent real'.

Unidentified flying objects (UFOs) are another interesting case to hand. Some people see them, but many don't. It may be that UFOs are 'real' for those who see them, but not for anyone else.

Descartes, as we have seen, said that he was able to doubt the reality both of the world and of his own physical body. Perhaps he was right. Perhaps we ought to take a leaf out of his book.

11: Limits to the Imagination

Imagination is more important than knowledge – Einstein

Before we go on to discuss a possible synthesis for how the world might be made, we need to go back to the subject of using our imagination. As we saw in the last chapter, it is sometimes desirable to ignore our own internal 'chatter' – which is invariably verbal by nature. We need to set language aside and try to visualize how things could conceivably be. As always, we will be running the risk of getting carried away by the excesses of our reverie, but – as we shall see – there are actual limits to what it is possible to imagine. First, however, it is useful to look at one or two fundamental concepts that most people tend to find quite elusive and difficult to imagine.

Nothing

Nothing – nothingness – is, by definition, the complete absence of anything and everything. It is the complete absence of the universe itself. To apply the concept of 'grades of reality' we saw in the last chapter, we would have to say that 'nothingness', in its absolute sense, is giving the universe a 'reality coefficient' of zero. We would normally tend to visualize this as a region of space (whether finite or infinite) that is completely black and empty – except that for it to be truly 'nothing' there cannot even be any space for it to be empty.

Scientists are already trying to address the question, *why is there something, rather than nothing?* Applying the principle of Occam's razor (which says that the simplest possible explanation for anything is most likely to be the right one) to the universe as a whole, they believe that, at the deepest level, the laws of physics are really very simple. But the simplest conceivable universe is one which doesn't exist, and in which nothing ever happens. Clearly the universe is not like this. Why not?

We have seen that, by definition, nothing is what doesn't exist. It is what isn't there. So what would be there if there were no universe? It would be a case of what is there is what *isn't* there. A contradiction. It would thus appear that there has to be *something* there just to resolve the contradiction. (The Greek philosopher Parmenides proposed a very similar argument more than two thousand years ago.)

Infinity

Another fundamental concept which boggles the mind is infinity. We have already encountered it in the chapter on mathematics, and we know that it is what we get if we try to divide any finite number by zero. But how can we visualize infinity? Strictly speaking, we can't. It is 'out there' somewhere, but it is so far off that we can only imagine viewing it from a distance – if, indeed, even that is possible. There is absolutely no way we could ever visualize anything being 'at' a distance of infinity.

The question of whether the universe is finite or infinite in extent raises conceptual difficulties in both cases. If we think, or if it turns out, that the universe is finite in extent (whether bounded or not) there is the vexing question of what might lie outside it. But if it is infinite in extent, we are faced with the question of what might be out there 'at' a distance of infinity, given that we can never observe it. Whatever the extent of the physical universe, it would seem that *space* (as one can best imagine it) is infinite – but that whatever might be 'out there' at an infinite distance cannot be observed and is therefore *not defined*.

Some scientists have seriously suggested that space might indeed be infinite in its extent, but that it might be filled with a *repeating pattern* of copies of a finite universe – similar to the patterns on wallpaper. The idea is an interesting one, but we have no way of knowing whether such a view is correct. There is no evidence that could help us decide.

We are faced with similar difficulties if we consider time to be infinite. Again, we cannot conceive of what might have happened an infinitely long time ago; nor can we imagine what might be happening infinitely far into the future.

Infinitesimals

An infinitesimal is a finite number which is as close to zero as we can possibly get – an 'infinitely small' amount, but not quite zero. Strictly speaking, there is no such thing as an infinitesimal, since however close to zero we can get, we can always get a bit closer. The concept of infinitesimals is closely linked to *Zeno's paradox* in which the hare (in theory) could never catch up with the tortoise because he would have to cross an infinite number of points in order to do so.

Infinitesimals figure strongly in the underlying theory of *calculus* (see Chapter 8) in which we examine what happens to the ratio $\Delta y/\Delta x$ as Δx (a tiny increment in the value of x) approaches zero. They occur also in *fractals.* In the example of the 'Koch snowflake', which we saw earlier, every 'straight' section of the figure boundary becomes 'infinitely small' as the figure develops.

Infinitesimals occur as a natural consequence of anything being smooth and continuous. However, as we saw in quantum theory, nothing in nature is smooth and continuous. It would appear that nature abhors infinitesimals. This is another example of how the laws of mathematics can 'work' in abstraction without showing any kind of physical manifestation.

Having often given my own imagination free rein (I wrote a fantasy trilogy before writing this book) and being introspective by nature, I can assure the reader that, in my lifetime, I've imagined all kinds of improbable events. Many of these would have been physically impossible (as far as we can tell) and a good few were downright ridiculous. However, in my mental wanderings, I have found that (in addition to the above) there are certain things which are absolutely *impossible* to imagine, and it is instructive to take note of what these are.

Firstly, I cannot imagine the laws of mathematics being any different from the ones we know. I can imagine worlds in which the laws of chemistry and physics are radically different from ours, but not so with mathematics. Two and two cannot be two and two if they do not add up to four. This is obvious but, at a deeper level, it reflects something fundamental about the nature of things. As we saw earlier, mathematical laws do not necessarily require any form of physical expression in order to be valid.

Secondly, I cannot imagine such a thing as an unobserved event. If I visualize something in my mind's eye, I automatically see myself in the role of observer. I cannot avoid this. Similarly, if I imagine a sound, a smell, a taste or other sensation, I am again putting myself in the role of an observer. What I cannot observe is indistinguishable from nothingness – and an unobserved universe is indistinguishable from one that does not exist. I can – and often do – envisage myself as a 'disembodied' observer. I have no difficulty over this. But I cannot imagine anything happening without my knowing.

Thirdly, if I try to imagine myself being another person (putting myself 'in their shoes', so to speak), my imagination starts to play a strange trick. I have no difficulty in seeing myself in that other person's body, wearing that person's clothes, thinking that person's thoughts and expressing myself as that person would. I can even imagine being an animal – especially if it a mammalian species not unlike our own. At the deepest level, however, it is the same 'I' that is taking the role of that other person or creature. No matter how I try, I can never envisage a different 'I' from myself. Neither can I imagine myself splitting into more than one entity. If I did, I would find myself seeing the world from the points of view of *all* of the component entities. But every one of them would be the same 'I' that is me.

It is thus perfectly legitimate for me to think that I may be the only observer in the whole universe. (A similar view has already been put forward by the retired American physicist Amit Goswami.) It has to be noted that if we assume this uniqueness of the observer then, in the scenario of the block universe, this eliminates the problem of 'now' being different for different observers. The principle of Occam's razor, as we have seen, states that, where there are alternative explanations for anything, the simplest one is most likely to be correct. In this context, the assumption that there is only one observer in the whole universe does indeed simplify the whole picture.

The reader is invited to ponder deeply over these questions, and to repeat these 'thought experiments' at leisure. I have tried my best to put linguistic considerations to one side in my ruminations, and these were the results I obtained. In the next chapter I shall try to put together what I consider to be a reasonable synthesis of how the universe might be made, but we first need a set of *Ground Rules* in order to do so. And so, having explored the limits to my own imagination, I propose the following:

The Ground Rules

1) The primaeval void is self-contradictory and cannot prevail.
2) All manifestation obeys simple laws as governed by the laws of mathematics.
3) The laws of mathematics are absolute and independent of any manifestation.
4) The reality of any manifestation is dependent upon it being observed.
5) The observer is singular and unique.
6) The observer exists *per se* and cannot be defined or

    explained in terms of anything else.

7 Subject to these conditions, the observer exercises free will.

In this context, 'manifestation' means any object, event or situation that is observed. The universe itself is thus a manifestation. Anything that is not observed is not a manifestation.

It will be useful at this point to expand upon the Ground Rules as stated here, and to explore their ramifications. We discussed the self-contradictory nature of nothingness earlier in this chapter, and so no further comment on it is needed here. Ground Rule 2 implies that the principle of Occam's Razor applies along with the laws of mathematics. Ground Rule 3 emphasizes the immutability of the laws of mathematics along with the fact that these are still valid even without any form of physical expression. Ground Rule 4 follows from the fact that one cannot imagine or visualize an unobserved object or event; one always has to include oneself in the picture – even if only as a 'disembodied' observer. Ground Rule 5 follows from what happens when we try to visualize ourselves in someone else's shoes. It also eliminates the contradictory nature of 'simultaneity' under the special theory of relativity. (The existence of multiple observers cannot be proved experimentally, but the principle of Occam's Razor implies that there need only be one.) Ground Rule 6 emphasizes the transcendent nature of conscious awareness (the essential property of the observer), while Ground Rule 7 allows for the observer having free will.

    Ground Rule 5 is possibly the most controversial assertion in the whole of this book, and I would not include it here if I were not certain of its correctness. I will not proselytize about the ramifications, and do not prescribe or predict how society might evolve in the light of such knowledge. Nor will I say whether this single observer is God – that is a matter of interpretation. What I can say here is that the uniqueness of the observer explains the transcendent nature of consciousness itself. It explains why we can never locate the 'seat of consciousness' in someone else's brain. It explains also why we can never ascertain what consciousness might 'look like', or what it might be 'made of'. Because *we* are the very thing that we are looking for.

(I am reminded here of a schoolboy trick in which one is asked to form a loop using one's forefinger and thumb, put one's other forefinger through the loop – and then try to catch it! This is the observer trying to observe itself!)

Ground Rule 7 suggests that we have free will *even if we live in a 'block universe' in which the future appears pre-ordained.* The fact that Morgan Robertson apparently foresaw the sinking of the *Titanic* some fourteen years before it actually happened strongly suggests a future that is pre-ordained. However, given that we have free will, we should perhaps say that the future is (figuratively speaking) set in modelling clay rather than stone.

Having mulled over these questions for much of my life, I am convinced that the Ground Rules, as expressed here, are correct, and that they form the basis of all existence. They ought to provide a sound base for all future scientific advancement. In the next chapter we shall examine how the Ground Rules may enable us to synthesize a new model of the universe.

12: Building a Universe

We saw in the previous chapter that primaeval nothingness contradicts itself by being both 'there' and 'not there', also that there has to be an observer in order to create the 'something' that is needed to resolve the contradiction. This is the starting point for our BIG project, namely, building a universe. Since the Ground Rules are of such fundamental significance, I will reiterate them here:

1) The primaeval void is self-contradictory and cannot prevail.
2) All manifestation obeys simple laws as governed by the laws of mathematics.
3) The laws of mathematics are absolute and independent of any manifestation.
4) The reality of any manifestation is dependent upon it being observed.
5) The observer is singular and unique.
6) The observer exists *per se* and cannot be defined or explained in terms of anything else.
7) Subject to these conditions, the observer exercises free will.

At the deepest level, primaeval nothingness and a single observer are all that is needed to start building our universe. In this context, the primaeval void is the 'nothing' and the observer is the 'something'. But the only thing the observer is able to observe at this point is – *nothing*. Something else is needed before the observer can start observing 'something'. As the observer is the only 'something' at this stage, it will, somehow, try to observe itself – which, of course, it cannot do. The nearest it can come to accomplishing this is to divide itself into *self* and *not-self*. It will then see itself as a 'something' which it can call 'me' looking at another 'something', which it calls 'not me'. Because the observer has created the not-self out of itself, however, *it will periodically swap places with it.* Alternatively, it could conceivably swap places with the void so that it is, effectively, nothing looking at something. The fact remains, however, that the observer must first create the 'something' out of itself in order to observe it.

Watching an ill-defined 'something' flash in and out of existence is hardly an interesting or meaningful occupation – except that this sequence of observations generates the flow of *time.* At this stage, time will be seen as a two-phase cycle – which may be interpreted as either linear or cyclic. It makes no difference which it is. To make things more interesting, the observer needs to create more than one 'something' – which it is able to do – but now there needs to be some provision for the 'somethings' to be seen simultaneously as *separate* objects. This leads to the creation of *space* – which starts initially as a line of objects (the 'somethings'). The line later folds upon itself in a zigzag manner to form a plane; then the plane similarly folds upon itself to form the three-dimensional space with which we are familiar. The objects which thus fill space now require a *shape,* and may be envisaged as fuzzy spheres (as this is the simplest shape). The space thus generated is not empty, but is filled with an array of microscopic objects, constantly swapping places as they flash in and out of existence.

The model we have so far constructed is identical to the quantized spacetime predicted by loop quantum gravity. The observer has thus created the one-dimensional 'space' which we normally call 'time' but which, for the purpose of this exercise, we may also call *temporal space.* The observer has also created the three-dimensional space which we normally call 'space' but which we could also call *spatial space.* (I will shortly introduce further 'spaces', hence this new terminology.)

The vision of myriads of microscopic particles (since this is what they are, now), flashing in and out of existence, still hardly seems interesting or purposeful. However, if space can be squeezed, stretched or otherwise distorted, things become yet more interesting. For this to be achieved, however, requires another space – a 'reference' space against which the distortions of the first space can be compared.

The new space to be added now has *seven* dimensions. This number may sound extravagant, but it allows for a wide variety of new 'particles' (or particle formations) to be generated from the elements generated in the previous spaces. It also allows for a variety of forces to act upon those particles – gravity and electromagnetism, for example. For want of a better name, I shall call this new space *e/m space*. (The *e/m* designation may refer either to energy and mass, or to electromagnetism – it doesn't matter which.) The addition of the seven dimensions of e/m space brings the number of dimensions up to eleven – the same number as predicted by loop quantum gravity.

Finally, the role of the observer is to *observe* as well as to manipulate what is happening. Observation is pointless, however, if what has been observed is instantly forgotten. The observer therefore needs a *memory* in which the results of observations may be stored. This 'memory space' may also function as a kind of scratch pad whereby the observer may test various ideas without letting them manifest physically. This fourth space is the *transcendental space* and has fifteen dimensions. It is conceivable that the observer might create further transcendental spaces if the need arises. However, to the best of our knowledge, the four spaces proposed here should be sufficient to describe the universe as we know it. Overall, we have created a universe of 26 dimensions.

In Chapter 2 we saw how the observer imposes a subjective 'preferred direction' (the 'hidden compass' phenomenon) on the landscape as perceived. Although the 'preferred direction' is not necessarily the same for every observer (assuming that there are more than one) and can sometimes 'shift', thus changing the appearance of the place, it is impossible for us to visualize what space must 'really' look like in the absence of a preferred direction. Since space (spatial space, in this instance) is, at the deepest level, generated by the observer, we must therefore assume that the presence of a 'preferred direction' is a *fundamental property* of spatial space and, arguably, of the higher order (e/m and transcendental) spaces, also.

Looking at these spaces mathematically, it is apparent that while the Cartesian co-ordinate system is easier to work with mathematically, the system of cylindrical polar co-ordinates provides a more accurate picture of how the various spaces evolve and are organized.

Note that the number of dimensions in each space is of the form $2^n - 1$, giving values of 1, 3, 7 and 15. Each space may accordingly be referred to by its *ordinal number* (n) as well as giving it a name like 'temporal'.

Note also that the Einsteinian notion of a 'spacetime' in which space and time are (at least partially) interchangeable has been extended from four to twenty-six dimensions. In this model, both time and space (spatial space) may also be partially interchangeable with any of the additional dimensions in the e/m and transcendental spaces.

To summarize, we have:
Temporal Space (1 dimension) which we experience as the succession of events which we call *time*.

Spatial Space (3 dimensions) which separates the objects and events which we observe at any given instant, and which we usually call *space*.

e/m Space (7 dimensions) which (ostensibly) manifests as the phenomena of energy and matter, and which probably includes the strong and weak nuclear forces, electromagnetism and (possibly) gravitation.

Transcendental Space (15 dimensions) which is 'hidden' from the physical world as we know it, but which may provide 'storage space' for the observer's memories, dreams, fantasies and ideas. It may also include alternate realities (parallel universes) which *may*, in exceptional circumstances, be perceived by the observer as *intrusions* into the manifested reality.

The first three of these spaces may be classed as *manifest spaces* as they relate to the conditions that are physically manifest. Transcendental space, however, relates to the mind of the observer and is thus hidden from the world as manifested externally.

Contemporary physicists regard the extra dimensions of e/m space as being 'rolled up very small', and most do not acknowledge the existence of a transcendental space. An alternative to this, however, is dimensions which 'hitch a ride' on other dimensions.

I can perhaps illustrate this idea by considering the scenario of a train which runs to a rigid schedule. It is known *exactly* what time the train will set off, how fast it will travel on any given point of the journey, and what time it will arrive at its destination. Provided that the train keeps to this schedule, we could legitimately place track-side markers along the track to indicate the time, while the driver could look at his watch to see how far the train has travelled. Thus the time dimension has 'hitched a ride' on one of the dimensions of spatial space (or *vice versa*). The spatial dimension, in this instance, would be the route taken by the train. According to relativity, these two dimensions will be partially interchanged – as is the case for any moving object.

For clarity, it may help if we give names to the 'particles' of the different spaces. The particle of time, as we saw in Chapter 5, is the *chronon* with a duration of approximately 10^{-43} seconds. The smallest length or distance in spatial space is the Planck length, which is approximately 10^{-35} metres; an 'atom' or 'grain' of spatial space may thus be envisaged as a sphere or cube (it doesn't matter which) with a 'diameter' of one Planck length. We could call this unit a *topon* (from the Greek word for *place*). The seven-dimensional 'atom' of e/m space we could call a *steron* (from the Greek word for *solid*) and the fifteen-dimensional 'atom' of transcendental space (if we can conceive of such a thing) may be dubbed a *crypton* (meaning *hidden*) – not to be confused with the chemical element of krypton.

Every point in this 26-dimensional manifold will thus be defined by 26 numbers, including one to define an instant in time, three to define its position in space, and seven to define its physical attributes. The remaining fifteen numbers (from transcendental space) do not refer to any physical attributes, but may refer to the observer's options for changing the conditions at that point – thus exercising free will. The manifesting spaces have, in total, eleven dimensions but, in transcendental space, there is a 'reserve' of a further fifteen dimensions. This is more than enough to create alternate realities, which could, from the observer's perspective, replace the existing reality. Such alternate realities may be interpreted as parallel universes or even a spirit world.

All of the dimensions in the 26-dimensional manifold are mutually interchangeable and, by substituting dimensions from the transcendental space for some or all of the dimensions in the manifest spaces, the observer may change the perceived physical environment completely. (The Phantom Guest House and the Palace of Versailles are cases which come to mind.) The observer will, however, always perceive the world as having a one-dimensional temporal space (the flow of time), a three-dimensional spatial space (the landscape) and a set of 'physical' phenomena as defined by the parameters of e/m space.

(It is conceivable that particles from the transcendental space could pop in and out of the manifest spaces – possibly giving rise to the uncertainties that are endemic in the quantum world.)

It must always be remembered, however, that the 'mind of the observer' creates *all* that is manifest, since without the observer there can be no universe at all. And one 'reality' is as good as any other.

Whilst I cannot offer a full explanation of the 'unexplained' phenomena as described in Chapters 1 and 2, it is apparent that my idea of a 15-dimensional 'transcendent space' may at least *begin* to offer an explanation. Much research remains to be done but, I suspect, this is potentially a promising lead.

13: The Physics of Astrology

We have now (in theory) built our universe. There are two essential properties of the observed universe which require special attention, however. One of these is that spatial space is almost certainly quantized, probably in the format of a three-dimensional square matrix; the other is a consequence of the general theory of relativity, namely, that the presence of a massive body in space distorts the space immediately surrounding it. This is analogous to a heavy ball bearing placed on top of a rubber sheet. It is the combination of these two factors that give rise to the physical phenomena which we interpret as 'astrology'. We thus have to consider the question of whether the positioning of large (planet-sized and larger) objects in spatial space has any effect on what happens here on Planet Earth.

Apparently the positioning of the planets, as seen from Earth, does have a subtle physical effect. The gravitational forces involved are too weak to account for this, but the quantization of space *may* account for it. In Chapter 6 we saw a possible analogy between pixellated space and a loosely woven dishcloth. Because of the 'cubic' spatial pattern, the 'fault lines' generated by each planet will be at right angles to each other. (We saw evidence of the pixellation of space, also, when we discussed gravitational lensing). When planets are positioned 90 or 180 degrees apart (as seen from the Earth), the fault lines themselves will become aligned, creating a measure of 'instability' in the vicinity of the Earth. It is this factor which apparently causes the 'hard aspects' of astrology to concur with 'difficult' times.

Also, in Chapter 3, we saw how an opposition between the planets Uranus and Neptune appeared to trigger the San Francisco earthquake of April 1906. Given what we now know about relativity and quantum mechanics, we now have a possible mechanism for how this might happen.

Let's Play a Game

As a little light relief from the 'heavy' philosophy we have been discussing in the foregoing sections, we can play a little 'game. Using pixellated space as a (physical) base, we can construct a 4x4 square matrix and then draw in the inscribed circle. Since the sine of an angle of 30 degrees (and the cosine of 60 degrees) is exactly one half, the cell boundaries will divide the circle into exactly twelve equal arc-lengths – the basis for the twelve signs of the zodiac. (See Fig.14a.) We can designate the central horizontal line in the diagram as the *horizon* and the central vertical as the *meridian*.

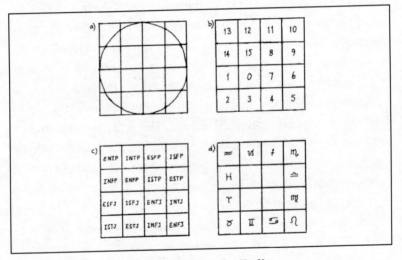

Fig. 14: Building the Zodiac:

a) Space quantization; b) The Walkaround; c) Myers-Briggs Profiles;
d) The Traditional Zodiac

We can take this further. Let us number the 16 small squares ('cells') in the diagram as shown in Figure 14b. Let us also imagine that this is a park and that we are going to take a walk around it, visiting each of the small squares in numerical order. We will imagine erecting a flagpole in each of the odd-numbered squares when we visit it, designating that cell with the letter I (representing the flagpole). We set off from Cell Zero and erect a flagpole in Cell 1. When we reach Cell 2 we have turned around and are now *returning to the meridian*. We will therefore label each of Cells 2 and 3 with the letter U – the curved shape of the letter representing this turnaround. In Cell 4 we are moving away from the meridian again, *but have started our climb back up to the horizon*. The next four cells are thus labelled with the letter O – the circular shape representing completion of the cycle. The cycle is repeated in the upper half of the diagram, and all eight of the upper cells are labelled with the letter S (for Sky). The twelve 'zodiac signs', around the periphery of the diagram, are thus labelled as follows:

Cell 1 (Aries) I
Cell 2: (Taurus) U
Cell 3: (Gemini) UI
Cell 4: (Cancer) O
Cell 5: (Leo) OI
Cell 6: (Virgo) OU
Cell 9: (Libra) SI
Cell 10: (Scorpio) SU
Cell 11: (Sagittarius) SUI
Cell 12: (Capricorn) SO
Cell 13: (Aquarius) SOI
Cell 14: (Pisces) SOU

What, if anything, does this tell us about the twelve signs of the zodiac? We could extend the symbolism further and say that I represents direction or thrust (equivalent to 'extroversion'), U represents enclosure, O represents the concentration or compaction of energies and S represents being out there in the real world (as it is above the horizon). Using this symbolism, we might thus interpret each zodiac sign as follows:

Aries: Primal force or thrust

Taurus: Enclosure – 'inside the box'

Gemini: Movement inside the box – short-range communications

Cancer: Concentration of energy

Leo: Release of concentrated energy

Virgo: Channelling of energy

Libra: Reactive force – restoring balance

Scorpio: 'Outside the box' – peeking into the unknown

Sagittarius: 'Reaching to the stars'

Capricorn: Nothing more to discover – pride mixed with disappointment

Aquarius: Visions of what might yet be

Pisces: The global city

By using a simple algorithmic approach we have effectively *built the signs of the zodiac from scratch.* (Pedantic astrologers may dispute the interpretations I have given to some of the signs, but the essential pattern is there.)

As a further corollary, we should note Hans Eysenck's observation that people born under the odd-numbered zodiac signs are significantly more extroverted than those born under the other six signs. Extroversion – Introversion (E-I) is, however, one of four scales used in the Myers-Briggs personality profiling system. The other three scales are Sensing – iNtuition (S-N); Feeling – Thinking (F-T) and Judging – Perceiving (J-P). There are exactly sixteen possible profiles under this system – and sixteen cells in the grid. It is thus *conceivable* that there could be correspondences between the Myers-Briggs profiles and the zodiac signs. Figure 14c shows one possible arrangement, although we ought not to accept this as being definitively correct. If this model is valid (which it may not be) then it is more likely that each zodiac sign will *tend* to favour certain Myers-Briggs profiles over others. Readers are invited to do their own research on this.

We agreed at the outset that this little exercise was only a game. *But is it?*

There is, of course, the small question of where in the sky the zodiac actually begins (assuming that the concept is a valid one). Western astrologers say that the zodiac starts from the vernal point – the intersection of the ecliptic with the celestial equator – a point, currently in the constellation of Pisces, but which drifts westward against the stellar background, due to the earth's precession. (The drift is about one degree every 72 years.) The ancients, however, based their zodiac on the constellations, claiming that it started at the 'first point' of the constellation of Aries – an arbitrary point in the sky, which does not even have a physical existence. A more logical place to start, possibly, is some bright star either on or very close to the line of the ecliptic. (It appears that Regulus was used for this purpose at one time – which would explain the naming of this star.) Another place from which the zodiac could be said to begin is the eastern horizon, which astrologers use as the basis for the *house system* – a secondary 'zodiac' which they use for forecasting mundane events.

The Music of the Spheres

The Signs of the Zodiac – if we accept them as a genuine property of spatial space – are just that. Divisions of space. The planets are different. They are huge lumps of matter which bend and distort space, and whose positions and alignments do, evidently, have some physical effect. We may ignore them if we wish, but they won't go away. Astrologers have long assigned to each planet a distinct 'personality', going so far as to name each one after a Roman god. (Saturn, paradoxically, is generally considered, in astrological terms, to wield more 'clout' than any other planet in the solar system – even though Jupiter is bigger, more massive and nearer to the Earth than Saturn is.)

Might there be a physical basis for this?

If these 'planetary principles' are indeed a genuine phenomenon, the best explanation I can offer is that space (spatial space) *oscillates* according to a complex pattern – possibly due to gravitational waves originating from the sun. Each planet could thus have a vibrational mode depending upon its distance from the sun. I would envisage this as a series of ripples emanating from the sun and spreading out in every direction. Saturn could thus wield more 'clout' than Jupiter simply by virtue of its location within this oscillatory pattern. It is conceivable that the same binary symbols which we used for delineating the Signs of the Zodiac might also be used to delineate a *possible* set of symbolic characteristics for each planet. We could, for example, have:

Binary code 0001 (I)	= The Earth or the Sun
" 0010 (U)	= The Moon
" 0011 (U + I)	= Mercury
" 0100 (O)	= Venus
" 0101 (O + I)	= Mars
" 0110 (O + U)	= Jupiter
" 0111 (O + U + I)	= Saturn
" 1000 (S)	= Uranus
" 1001 (S + I)	= Neptune
" 1010 (S + U)	= Pluto

Each planet is thus assigned the same code as one of the zodiac signs – which may explain why astrologers claim that certain planets 'rule' particular signs. The example used here, while it shows how planets *might* have affinities with certain zodiac signs, is for illustrative purposes only. It is purely speculative and does *not* agree the traditional pattern of 'rulerships' used by practising astrologers. More research needs to be done on this.

Angles and Aspects

As observed from the earth, the positions of the sun, moon and planets are seen to change over time. We have already seen that, while their positioning within the constellations is of no physical significance, there is evidence that the *angles* subtended by each pair of bodies (as seen from Earth) is significant, due to space quantization. The fabric of space is thus analogous to a loosely woven dishcloth, and the presence of large (planet-sized) bodies within it causes it to 'tear'. It is equivalent to pushing a pencil into the fabric. When the planetary bodies are in straight alignment or positioned at angles of 90 or 180 degrees, these tears or fault-lines in space line up and have a destabilizing effect on the locality thus affected. Where space is 'torn' in this way there is potential trouble – but this passes once the planets have moved away from such an alignment.

While many, if not most, scientists remain sceptical about the validity of any kind of astrologically based paradigm – and are likely to remain so for the foreseeable future – we already have sufficient evidence to show that the laws of physics can and probably do account for at least *some* of the types of phenomena which we class as 'astrology'. Space quantization and the general theory of relativity, when combined, are all that we need to find an explanation.

If it eventually turns out that the theory of loop quantum gravity was wrong and that space is smooth and continuous after all, then the conclusion has to be that astrology doesn't work. If such is the case, then we may be justified in concluding that astrology was a hoax all along, and that the matter ends there. Current evidence suggests that space *is* quantized or pixellated, however, which does indeed provide a credible basis for the kinds of phenomena which we class as 'astrology'. If, in the end, it turns out that there is some astrological paradigm that can be *demonstrated* to work – even if it differs from traditional astrology

– then there will be some general *laws* of astrology, deriving from the laws of physics, which apply throughout the whole universe and not just our own little solar system. Watch this space.

14: The Making of Man

We have built our universe, but we have yet to put ourselves into the picture. We have built the stage; it is time to put the actors in it. The 'universe' we have built so far is a credible model, but one in which we merely 'exist' as disembodied observers. Except – as we have seen from the Ground Rules – there is really just *one* observer.

Somehow this observer needs to create some kind of physical *persona* for itself so that it may interact directly with the physical 'reality' that it has created. Never forget, as we reflect upon this, that this single observer is *you* – and me – and all other sentient creatures throughout the universe.

The primaeval, 'disembodied' observer can be anywhere or, indeed, everywhere all at once. But it didn't create a universe just to look at it. The universe, thus created, is like a board-game, set up and ready for play. But the game has yet to begin. It first it needs some players.

Starting from its initial 'disembodied' condition, the observer first contracts to a single *point* in space (spatial space) to become a *point observer*, as opposed to an 'extended' one filling all of space. It then manipulates the time dimension (temporal space) so that this changes from a closed loop to a *spiral*. (The ancient Celts often used this image in their artwork – perhaps they knew something that we have since forgotten.) The observer is then able to look at the parallel 'time-lines' thus generated and see images of itself – which look and behave – and are interpreted – as 'other' observers. For clarity, we will simply call them the *Others* (with a capital 'O').

In the next stage, the observer identifies the region of space immediately surrounding it as *me-space*, the space outside it thus becoming 'not-me' space. (The Others identify their own me-spaces, also.) At this stage, the me-space will be amorphous and malleable. Empty space cannot interact directly with the space surrounding it, however, therefore something more is needed. The observer creates vortices within its me-space, which in turn start to generate the extra dimensions that make up e/m space. These vortices condense into fine particles (neutrinos?) which gradually fill up the me-space, making it denser than the surrounding space. At this level of development, the observer may be able to interact 'physically' with the Others, but not necessarily with other objects within the universe. For this, a still denser 'body' is needed. The observer is able to continue to fill up its me-space with more particles, and also with *electric and magnetic fields*. A stronger type of interaction is now possible, both with the Others and (possibly) with some physical objects in space. But any interactions with physical objects (made from *baryonic* matter – protons, neutrons and electrons) will nevertheless still be weak. The observer thus needs to build for itself a *baryonic body* in order for it to be able to engage properly with the baryonic stuff which we call the *physical* world. (The development of *all* living organisms follows a similar pattern.)

The baryonic forms which the observer may assume are initially very simple: they include viruses, bacteria and algae. Later, some of these evolve into more advanced plant forms, and also into simple animal forms. (There is little fundamental difference between the plant and animal forms at this level: they are all *living* organisms.) Eventually, more and more advanced animal forms evolve, including fish, amphibians, reptiles, birds, mammals and – ultimately – humans.

Baryonic matter has disadvantages, however. It is cumbersome and has to be carried around during the entire lifetime of the organism. It is also subject to a process of continual attrition. Baryonic ('physical') entities are assaulted on a daily basis by mechanical forces and chemical agents until they finally cease to be viable. At this point, it becomes necessary for the observer to discard its old baryonic shell, either to seek a new one or just to become free again. This is the process we interpret as 'death and rebirth'.

Mystics and others have often talked of man as having not a single body (which they call the 'physical' body) but also an *etheric body,* an *astral body* and a *mental body.* Applying the model we have just developed here, we could equate the 'etheric body' with the electromagnetic matrix, which, as we saw in Chapter 7, underlies the transmission of nerve impulses. The 'astral body' may be accounted for by a concentration of finer particles (probably neutrinos) permeating the physical organism; and the 'mental body' corresponds to what we might call the 'me-space'. The baryonic shell is, of course, what we call the 'physical body' or just the 'body'. During the lifetime of the 'physical' organism, all of these 'bodies' interpenetrate one another and function as a single unit. When the baryonic part of the organism is no longer functioning, however, it is discarded. The remaining 'bodies' filter out of it and continue to function without it.

It is very sad that, when this inevitably happens, those who are left in the baryonic world (the 'earth plane' as it is sometimes called) see only the discarded baryonic shell of the organism. They cannot see or sense the invisible and intangible parts of the organism which have been freed and which have gone elsewhere – or which may still be hovering around. It has been noted on many occasions that a dying person loses a small amount of mass at the moment of death – always the same amount, stated (subject to confirmation) to be 21 grams. This is evidence of some rarefied material leaving the 'physical' body.

And what of the subjective experiences of the observer as it creates 'bodies' for itself, inhabits them for a while and then discards them? Observation is somewhat pointless unless the experiences are remembered – and thus *stored* somewhere. This is why the extra dimensions of the transcendental space are so important. The observer's bank of stored memories is what may be interpreted as the *soul* of the observer. (It is different from *spirit* in that the latter is simply the observer itself.) The extra dimensions accommodate not only the observer's memories, but also alternative visions of worlds which do not exist but which could yet be. It is the observer's memories which provide the raw material for this. And it is the observer's choice whether to make any of these alternative worlds a reality.

At the beginning of its sequence of incarnations the observer will know nothing. It will have remembered nothing, and so will have to observe everything in order to learn. At first it will only be able to assimilate very simple experiences, but the memories of these will be laid down in the transcendental space, and will subsequently become *knowledge*. Knowledge as such is simply *the memories upon which predictions about the future may be based*. (As an example, I can *predict* what the city of Oxford will look like on my next visit because I have been there before, and have *remembered* what the city looked like from previous visits.) Images of everything observed are *reproduced* in the transcendental space, to be accessed again (at leisure) by the observer. Sometimes it appears that the contents of the transcendental space can intrude into the 'physical' space which we normally accept as the reality – which may account for the phantom armies seen at Edgehill, and the non-existent guest houses encountered at Boscastle and Montélimar. More likely, however, is that the observer sometimes 'tunes into' such alternate realities.

The imagery held in the transcendental space may also be accessible to the Others – thus accounting for the phenomena of telepathy.

As the observer builds up more and more memories, it is able to build for itself increasingly complex organisms which it can then inhabit, and so engage in ever more complex types of experience. Even plant life has its own experiences, as well as (believe it or not) so-called 'inanimate' matter. The most complex experiences of all are those which we ourselves enjoy (or endure), as humans.

It has sometimes been suggested by theologians and others that animals *share* their memories (a *hive soul*), but that humans do not. It may be that the sheer scale and complexity of human experience necessitates both a much larger brain and individualized memory banks, as opposed to a hive soul.

The incarnate observer almost invariably forgets that the Others (both people and animals) are simply incarnations of itself on parallel time-tracks. The Others all compete with the observer for resources, unaware that the 'winner' will be the 'loser' when it returns to the present time on a different time-track. Again, I will not proselytize over this.

The Naming of Parts

In the light of these discussions, we are now in a position to update some of the terminology we have traditionally used in theology and philosophy. Thus we now have:

Spirit: the observer

Soul: the observer's accumulated memories over a series of lifetimes

Hive Soul: memories shared by individuals of the same species

Mind: the assimilation and processing of experiences

Persona: the vehicle whereby the observer becomes 'visible' to 'other' observers

Body: the tangible part of the persona, which can interact with its physical surroundings

Universe: the totality of everything observed or implied to exist

World: another name for the Universe

Heaven: an idealized world, unobservable from the physical plane but possibly existing as a parallel world in the transcendent space

Infinite Soul: the totality of *all* memories from *all* organisms

Akhashic Records: another name for the Infinite Soul
God: the observer in its fully evolved state when it has instant
   access to the Akhashic Records

We are all on this roller-coaster journey which we call 'life' or 'the world'. We have long tried to understand it, usually with varying success. As we observe the world, we learn. We try things, we make mistakes – and we learn. As our memories build up, we increase our knowledge and awareness of the world around us. At this particular time in history, many of us are worrying that we may be in the process of destroying the planet, either by warfare or by industrial pollution. But the learning process must continue regardless. If the worst happens and we render the planet uninhabitable, we will find (or be given) another one where (hopefully) we can do less damage. Having destroyed a planet that was once one's home will then, undoubtedly, be a major lesson learnt. Whatever happens, the learning process must – and will – continue indefinitely. Ultimately we will evolve to a point where we no longer need 'physical' bodies, and our memories will merge into the great database in the sky (or wherever) – which some call the *Akhashic Records*.

How much of this scenario is likely to be real? Of, course, I cannot actually *prove* any of it. Each of us has his or her own reality. All experience is valid, however. At some stage in the *very* distant future – many, many times the lifetime of the universe into the future – when we have already learnt everything – it is conceivable that *we may forget it all,* just so that we can start over again. Why? Because, having known everything for a long time, we may become stale. We may become bored with it all. And so we will forget everything – just so that we can maintain interest by starting the learning cycle all over again.

At the most fundamental level, however, there are only two things – primaeval nothingness (which doesn't exist) – and the single observer. This is how it always was. Everything that follows is a result of the interaction between these two. And, as always, the laws of mathematics define what is possible.

Postscript

No one asked me to write this book. So why did I do it? The world has long needed a book like this one but, until now, no one had written one. And so – at the risk of becoming famous – I chose to write it myself. This has by no means been an onerous task, however. On the contrary, I have felt strongly motivated in this endeavour.

Like many before me, I have long enquired into the nature of the cosmos, of reality and of my own place within it. Before I retired, I used to teach physics, a subject which has much to say about the nature of things. To the best of my ability I taught my students a view of the world based upon our (then) current understanding of the laws of physics. But again, as I said in Chapter 2, even scientists dream. On numerous occasions I have had first-hand experience of things which simply do not make sense, given our present knowledge and understanding of the laws of physics. And these were not just personal experiences like dreams. Some of the things I have seen – notably at spirit séances – have been witnessed by many besides myself.

Also, we must never lose sight of the fact that, at one time, phenomena such as earthquakes and thunderstorms were unexplained and deemed to be the work of capricious deities.

In the introduction to this book I referred to three approaches to interpreting the nature of the reality in which we live: the Shamanic approach; the Scriptural approach – and the Scientific approach. By far, the Scientific approach has been the most successful enterprise yet in uncovering the mysteries of nature. It has already built a firm foundation upon which we can build a realistic model of the universe and its workings. So far, however, in building this model, we have omitted our own role as the observer.

As scientific knowledge has advanced, the role of the observer in nature has increasingly become more important. In classical physics, the observer – assuming there was one there at all – was a mere spectator to everything that happened. And in quantum physics, it is now accepted that the observer has some influence over what happens at the subatomic level, but it isn't properly understood why this should be the case. Finally, in *Ultimum Mysterium*, we have seen evidence that the observer could be the very reason why everything exists in the first place.

In this book I have tried to paint the bigger picture. It includes modern science – it has to – but it also tries to fill the gaps that science has left behind. It tries to peek beyond the boundaries of what we normally call 'science'. Many scientists will, no doubt, be chagrined at some of the things I have turned up here. This is a regrettable, but inevitable phase. As ever, the onward march of discovery must go on. There is yet a vast 'hidden' universe that lies beyond the obvious, still waiting to be discovered. And what an adventure this will be!

As yet there are many gaps in my own knowledge of the world and, at best, I can only drop hints at what we may find. A book like this one obviously cannot cover every possibility. Such an enterprise would be a vast undertaking, which could culminate in a work the size of the *Encyclopaedia Britannica*. One thing is certain, however. The best is yet to come.

Further Reading

Albert, David Z and Galchen, Rivka, *A Quantum Threat to Special Relativity*, (Scientific American, March 2009, p26)

Al Khalili, Jim, *Paradox*, (Bantam Press, 2012)

Al Khalili, Jim, *Quantum: A Guide for the Perplexed*, (Weidenfeld & Nicholson, 2003)

Ambjørn, Jan et al, *The Self-Organizing Quantum Universe*, (Scientific American, July 2008, p24)

Atkinson, Sam (Ed), *The Philosophy Book*, (Dorling Kindersley, 2011)

Baez, John C and Huerta, John, *The Strangest Numbers in String Theory*, (Scientific American, May 2011, p44)

Baker, Alan, *The Edge of Science*, (Mainstream Publishing Company, 2009)

Baker, Joanne, *50 Quantum Physics Ideas*, (Quercus, 2013)

Balibar, Françoise, *Einstein: Decoding the Universe*, (Thames & Hudson, 2005)

Barrow, John D, *New Theories of Everything*, (Oxford University Press, 2007)

Bern, Zvi et al, *Loops, Trees and the Search for New Physics*, (Scientific American, May 2012, p20)

Bojowald, Martin, *Follow the Bouncing Universe*, (Scientific American, October 2008, p28)

Boslough, John, *Beyond the Black Hole*, (Collins, 1985)

Bousso, Raphael and Polchinski, Joseph, *The String Theory Landscape*, (Scientific American, September 2004, p60)

Brown, Elizabeth, *Dowsing*, (Hay House, 2010)

Capra, Fritjof, *The Tao of Physics*, (Wildwood House, 1975)

Carroll, Sean M, *The Cosmic Origins of Time's Arrow*, (Scientific American, June 2008, p26)

Carter, Chris, *Science and Psychic Phenomena*, (Inner Traditions, 2007, 2012)

Carter, Rita, *The Brain Book*, (Dorling Kindersley, 2009)

Carton, Steven (Ed), *Science But Not As We Know It*, (Dorling Kindersley, 2015)

Cave, Peter, *Philosophy*, (Oneworld, 2012)

Cheney, Margaret, *Tesla – Man Out of Time*, (Dell Publishing, 1981)

Chown, Marcus, *Quantum Theory Cannot Hurt You*, (Joseph Henry Press, 2006; Faber & Faber, 2007)

Clark, Jerome, *Unexplained!*, (Visible Ink Press, 1993)

Clegg, Brian, *Gravity*, (St Martin's Press, 2012)

Clegg, Brian, *Infinity* (Constable & Robinson, 2003)

Clifton, Timothy and Ferreira, Pedro, *Does Dark Energy Really Exist?*, (Scientific American, April 2009, p32)

Close, Frank, *Antimatter*, (Oxford University Press, 2009)

Close, Frank, *The Cosmic Onion*, (Heinemann Educational Books, 1983)

Costardi, Moheb, *50 Human Brain Ideas*, (Quercus, 2013)

Cox, Brian & Forshaw, Jeff, *The Quantum Universe: Everything That Can Happen Does Happen*, (Allen Lane, 2011)

Davies, Paul, *Other Worlds*, (Dent, 1980)

Davies, Paul, *The Goldilocks Enigma*, (Allen Lane, 2006)

Davis, Tamara M, *Is the Universe Leaking Energy?*, (Scientific American, July 2010, p20)

Dawkins, Richard, *The Magic of Reality*, (Black Swan, 2012)

Dunne, J W, *An Experiment with Time*, (Hampton Roads Publishing Company Inc; First published in 1927)

Du Sautoy, Marcus, *The Number Mysteries*, (Harper Collins, 2010)

Eigen, Manfred and Winkler, Ruthild, *Laws of the Game*, (R Piper & Co, Germany, 1975; English Translation: Allen Lane, 1982)

Ellis, George R, *Does the Multiverse Really Exist?* (Scientific American, August 2011, p18)

Emoto, Masaru, *The Hidden Messages in Water*, (Beyond Words Publishing Inc, 2001)

Fanthorpe, Lionel and Patricia, *Mysteries and Secrets of Time*,

(Dundurn, Toronto, 2007)

Fayer, Michael D, *Absolutely Small*, (Amacom, 2010)

Feynman, Richard P, *Easy & Not-So-Easy Pieces*, (Addison Wesley Longman, 1995 and 1997)

Forman, Joan, *The Mask of Time*, (MacDonald and Jane's, 1978)

Frank, Adam, *About Time*, (Simon & Schuster, 2011)

Freiberger, Marianne & Thomas, Rachel, *Numericon*, (Quercus, 2014)

Frissell, Bob, *Nothing in This Book Is True, But It's Exactly How Things Are*, (Frog Ltd Books, distr. by North Atlantic Books, 1994)

Gaunt, Bonnie, *Beginnings – The Sacred Design*, (Adventures Unlimited Press, 2000)

Gilkes, Ron, *Our Eternal Consciousness*, (Archer Press, 2009)

Gilliland, Ben, *How to Build a Universe*, (Philip's, 2015)

Gleiser, Marcelo, *The Island of Knowledge*, (Basic Books, 2014)

Goswami, Amit, *The Self-Aware Universe*, (Simon & Schuster, 1993)

Greene, Brian, *The Future of String Theory*, (Scientific American, November 2003, p48)

Gribbin, John, *In Search of Schrödinger's Cat*, (Wildwood House, 1984)

Gribbin, John, *Timewarps*, (Dent, 1979)

Gribbin, Mary & John, *The Science of Philip Pullman's 'His Dark Materials'*, (Hodder Children's Books, 2003)

Grieveson, Andrea, *Read How We Died*, (Con-Psy Publications, 1996)

Hale-Evans, Ron, *Mind Performance Hacks*, (O'Reilly, 2006)

Hamilton, David R, *Is Your Life Mapped Out?*, (Hay House, 2012)

Hammack, Edward O, Jr, *Complete Book of Practical Astrology*, (Parker Publishing Company Inc, New York, 1980)

Hawking, Stephen, *A Brief History of Time*, (Bantam Press, 1988)

Hawking, Stephen, *The Universe in a Nutshell*, (Bantam Press,

2001)

Hawking, Stephen and Penrose, Roger, *The Nature of Space and Time*, (Princeton University Press, 1996)

Heagarty, N Riley, *The French Revelation*, (Morris Publishing, 2000)

Heathcote-James, Emma, *After-Death Communication*, (Metro Publishing, 2003)

Heathcote-James, Emma, *They Walk Among Us*, (Metro Publishing, 2004)

Hedges, Patricia, *Understanding Your Personality*, (Sheldon Press, 1993)

Jones, Marie D and Flaxman, Larry, *11: The Time Prompt Phenomenon*, (Career Press, 2009)

Jones, Marie D and Flaxman, Larry, *This Book is from the Future*, (Career Press, 2012)

Kaku, Michio, *Physics of the Impossible*, (Doubleday, 2008)

Kaufmann, William J, *The Cosmic Frontiers of General Relativity*, (Little, Brown and Company, 1977)

Keirsey, David and Bates, Marilyn, *Please Understand Me*, (Gnosology Books Ltd., 1984)

Koch, Christof and Tononi, Giulio, *A Test for Consciousness*, (Scientific American, June 2011, p26)

Kosteletský, Alan, *The Search for Relativity Violations*, (Scientific American, September 2004, p74)

Krauss, Laurence M, *A Universe From Nothing*, (Free Press, 2012)

Lao Tzu, *Tao Te Ching*, (Traditional text – Various publishers)

Lineweaver, Charles H and Davis, Tamara M, *Misconceptions about the Big Bang*, (Scientific American, March 2005, p24)

Lykken, Joseph and Spiropulu, Maria, *Supersymmetry and the Crisis in Physics*, (Scientific American, May 2014, p22)

MacDonald, Matthew, *Your Brain – The Missing Manual*, (O'Reilly, 2008)

McLuhan, Robert, *Randi's Prize*, (Matador, 2010)

Mangabeira, Roberto & Smolin, Lee, *The Singular Universe and the*

Reality of Time, (Cambridge University Press, 2015)

Martin, Brian R, *Particle Physics,* (Oneworld Publications, 2011)

Mills, Robert, *Space Time and Quanta,* (Freeman & Company, New York, 1994)

Mitchell, John, *How the World is Made – Sacred Geometry,* (Thames & Hudson, 2009)

Moody, Dr Raymond, *Life After Life,* (MBB, 1975)

Moyer, Michael, *Is Space Digital?* (Scientific American, February 2012, p20)

Muldoon, Sylvan and Carrington, Hereward, *The Projection of the Astral Body,* (Rider, 1929)

Musser, George, *Was Einstein Right?* (Scientific American, September 2004, p70)

Nielsen, Michael A, *Rules for a Complex Quantum World,* (Scientific American, November 2002, p48)

Palffy, Georgina, *The Science Book,* (Dorling Kindersley, 2014)

Papineau, David, *Philosophical Devices,* (Oxford University Press, 2012)

Parkyn, Chetan, *Human Design,* (Harper Collins, 2009)

Peake, Anthony, *Is There Life After Death?* (Arcturus Publishing, 2009)

Peake, Anthony, *The Out-of-Body Experience,* (Watkins Publishing, 2011)

Penrose, Roger, *Cycles of Time,* (Bodley Head, 2010)

Penrose, Roger, *The Emperor's New Mind,* (Oxford University Press, 1989)

Penrose, Roger, *The Road to Reality,* (Jonathan Cape, 2004)

Pickover, Clifford A, *A Beginner's Guide to Immortality,* (Avalon, 2007)

Pickover, Clifford A, *The Physics Book,* (Sterling, 2011)

Pickover, Clifford A, *Time – A Traveller's Guide,* (Oxford University Press, 1998)

Pringle, Lucy, *Crop Circles,* (Pitkin Guides, 2006)

Quigg, Chris, *The Coming Revolutions in Particle Physics,* (Scientific

American, February 2008, p38)

Radin, Dean, *The Noetic Universe,* (Harper Collins, 1997)

Randall, Lisa, *Warped Passages,* (Allen Lane, 2005)

Randles, Jenny, *Time Storms,* (Piatkus, 2001)

Robinson, Andrew (Ed), *The Scientists,* (Thames & Hudson, 2012)

Rucker, Rudy, *Infinity and the Mind,* (Harvester Press, 1982)

Russell, Peter, *The Brain Book,* (Routledge & Kegan Paul, 1979)

Sagan, Carl, *The Cosmic Connection,* (Anchor Press, 1973)

Scientific American (Special Issue), *A Matter of Time,* (September 2002, reissued November 2006)

Sheldrake, Rupert, *The Science Delusion,* (Hodder & Stoughton, 2012)

Singh, Jagjit, *Modern Cosmology,* (Constable, 1961; Revised version: Penguin Books, 1970)

Smolin, Lee, *Atoms of Space and Time,* (Scientific American, January 2004, p56)

Smolin, Lee, *Time Reborn,* (Allen Lane, 2013)

Solomon, Grant & Jane, *The Scole Experiment,* (Piatkus, 1999)

Southwell, Gareth, *50 Philosophy Ideas,* (Quercus, 2013)

Steinhardt, Paul J, *The Inflation Debate,* (Scientific American, April 2011, p18)

Stemman, Roy, *Reincarnation,* (Piatkus, 1997)

Stewart, Ian, *Taming the Infinite,* (Quercus, 2008)

Stewart, Ian, *17 Equations that Changed the World,* (Profile Books, 2012)

Tart, Charles T, Puthoff, Harold E and Targ, Russell (Eds), *Mind at Large,* (Hampton Roads, 1979, 2002)

Tegmark, Max, *Our Mathematical Universe,* (Allen Lane, 2014)

Tegmark, Max, *Parallel Universes,* (Scientific American, May 2003, p30)

Thomas, Lewis, *The Lives of a Cell,* (Viking Press, 1974)

Thompson, John, *Nature's Watchmaker,* (Blackhall Publishing, 2009)

Tong, David, *The Unquantum Quantum,* (Scientific American,

December 2012, p32)

Tyrrell, G N M, *The Personality of Man*, (Pelican Books, 1946)

Vedral, Vlatko, *Decoding Reality*, (Oxford University Press, 2010)

Vedral, Vlatko, *Living in a Quantum World*, (Scientific American, June 2011, p20)

Veneziano, Gabriele, *The Myth of the Beginning of Time*, (Scientific American, May 2004, p30)

Von Baeyer, Hans Christian, *Quantum Weirdness? It's All in Your Mind*, (Scientific American, June 2013, p38)

Waddington, C H, *Tools for Thought*, (Paladin, 1977)

Walter, Katya, *Tao of Chaos*, (Element Books, 1994)

Wambach, Helen, *Life Before Life*, (Bantam Books, 1979)

Wambach, Helen, *Reliving Past Lives*, (Hutchinson, 1979)

Whitelaw, Ian, *A Measure of All Things*, (Quid Publishing, 2007)

Wilson, Colin and Grant, John (Eds), *The Directory of Possibilities*, (Webb & Bower, 1981)

Wolf, Fred Alan, *Parallel Universes*, (Touchstone, 1990)

Index

Abacus, 110

Agra (India), 32

Air ionizers, 49

Akhashic Records, 172

Algae, 168

Algebra, 116

Andrade, Hernami Guimares, 32

Andropov, Yuri, 47-8

An Experiment with Time, 81

Angular momentum (*see* Momentum – angular)

Animals, 52-3, 77-8, 101, 107-8

Anthropic principle, 99

Antimatter, 93

Archimedes, 138

Aries, 57, 161, 162

Aristotle, 129, 138

Artificial intelligence, 112-3

Aspects (astrology), 59-60, 159, 165

Astral body (*see* Body – astral)

Astrology, 56-64, 97, 159-66

Atoms, 132, 138

Austria, 50

Axon, 103

Babbage, Charles, 110

Bacteria, 168

Banbury, 10,53,85

Barbour, Julian, 88

Barrett, WF, 10, 12

BASIC, 111

Bedfordshire, 14

Bell, John, 92

" theorem, 92

Bélmez faces, 37-8

Bentham, Jeremy, 139

Benzene, 44

Bergmann, Peter, 88

Berne, 142

Big Bang, 79-80, 134

Big Bounce, 80, 134

Binary notation, 116

Bishop Auckland, 44-5

Black body radiation, 90

Black holes, 86-7, 133

Block universe, 83, 89, 94, 128, 151

Body:

" 'astral', 169

" baryonic ('physical'), 168-9

" 'etheric' ('light'), 104, 169

" 'mental', 169

Bohemia, 49

Boscastle, 12-13, 143, 170

Brain, 40, 104-9, 128

" reptilian, 107

Brainstem, 106-8

Branes, 95

Braud, William, 70

Broca's area, 104

Buddhism, 139
Butterfly effect, 124-5

Calculating devices, 110
Calculus, 122
Candle in the Wind, 42
Cartesian co-ordinates, 120
Cartoons, 113
Casimir, Hendrik, 97
" effect, 97, 133
Cellular automata, 125-6
Cerebellum, 106
Cerebrum, 104-5
Challenger shuttle disaster, 48
Chaos theory, 124-5
Chess, 98
Chronons (*see* Planck time)
Churchill, Winston, 58
Clocks, 76-7, 142
COBOL, 111
Colliculus:
" inferior, 107
" superior, 107
Compass, 'Hidden' (*see* Hidden
Compass phenomenon)
Compass, Magnetic, 54
Computation, 115-6
Computers, 110-3
Consciousness, seat of, 109-10
Constellations, 56
Continental drift, 6
Conway, HA, 125
Co-ordinate systems, 120
Copernicus, 130

Cornwall, 12-13
Corpus callosum, 105
Cottingley 'fairies', 7
Crookes, William, 66
Crop circles, 35, 36-7
'Cryptons', 157
Cycles of Time, 80

Dalai Lama, 33-4
Daniel, Book of, 20-1
Dark matter, 133
Darwin, Charles, 130
Dawkins, Richard, 66
Death, 169
De Broglie, Louis, 92
Democritus, 138
Dendrites, 103
Descartes, René, 107, 120, 138-9,
144
Devil, 8, 36
Devil's hoof marks, 35-6
Devon, 35-6
De Witt, Bryce, 88
Diana, Princess, 42
Differential equations, 122
Differentiation, 122
Dimensional analysis, 119-20
Dimensions, 85, 95-6, 134-5,
154, 156-7
Dirac, Paul, 93
Disorientation, 51-2
Doppler shift, 79
Dowsing, 53-4
Dreams, 15-16, 17-20, 44-9

" lucid, 44
Druidry, 2
Dualism, 139
Dunne, JW, 18-20, 81

Earth (planet), 82, 172
Earthquakes, 1, 6, 60-1, 159
" San Francisco (1906), 60-1
Ectoplasm, 66
Edgehill, Battle of, 9-10, 170
Edison, Thomas, 130
Einstein, Albert, 3, 76-7, 82, 90, 92, 130, 145
'Einstein cross', 84
Electricity, 101, 132
Electromagnetism, 101-2, 132
Electrons, 94, 99
Elementary particles (see Particles, elementary)
Ellison, Arthur, 39
Energy, 119
Entanglement, 92, 128
Escher, MC, 140
ESP (see Extra-sensory perception)
Ether (luminiferous), 82
Etheric body (see Body – etheric)
Euclid, 120, 138
Everett, Hugh, 99
Exponential:
" coefficient (e), 117
" expansion, 80
Extra-sensory perception (ESP), 67-70
Eysenck, Hans, 56-7, 162

Faraday, Michael, 101
Feynman, Richard, 94, 100
" diagrams, 94
Fibonacci series, 117-8
File-drawer problem, 73
Flight 191, 17-18
Fontana, David, 39
FORTRAN, 111
Four elements, 138
Fractals, 123-4
Frame dragging, 96, 133
Franklin, Benjamin, 6
Free will, 150, 152
Futility, 16-17

Galileo, 6, 130
Game of Life (see 'Life', Game of)
Ganzfeld experiments, 70
Gateshead, 54
Gauquelin, Michel, 56, 57
Gaussian distribution, 71-2
Gender, 34, 58
Geodesics, 120
Geometry, 120-1
Gight Castle, 8
God, 2, 172
Golden ratio (Φ), 117
Gorbachev, Mikhail, 59
Goswami, Amit, 149
Grand National horse race, 48-9,

64
Graphs, 121
Gravitation, 56, 79
Gravitational constant (G), 85, 120
Gravitational lensing, 84, 159
Great Year, 80
Greeks (ancient), 80, 129-30, 138
Ground Rules, 149-50, 152, 167
Gurney, Edmund, 66, 67
Gyroscopes, 131

Hagberry Pot, 8
Hammack, Edward O, Jr, 57-9
Haunting, 67
Hawking, Stephen80, 133
" radiation, 133
Heaven, 171
Heisenberg, Werner, 92
Heuristic programming (*see* Programming, heuristic)
'Hidden compass' phenomenon, 51-3, 141, 154-5
Higgs boson, 93
Hilbert, David, 121
Hippocampus, 106, 108
Hitler, Adolf, 58-9
Hive soul, 171
Honorton, Charles, 70
Houses (astrology), 163
Human Design, 61-3
Hydrogen atom, 85

I Ching, 62

Imagination, 141-2, 145-51
" limits, 145-9
Infinitesimals, 147
Infinite soul, 171
Infinity, 118, 146-7
Io, 23
Iteration, 122-4

Jenny's Sanctuary, 50
John, Elton, 42
Jourdain, Eleanor Frances, 10-11
Jupiter, 22-3, 57, 60, 163

Keen, Montague, 39
Kekulé, August, 44
Kennedy, John F, 41
Kineton, 10
Kitt Peak Observatory, 69
Koans, 139
Koch 'snowflake', 123
Krakatoa, 18
Krakower, Alan, 61-3

Laithwaite, Eric, 131
Language, 139, 140-1
" programming, 111
Large Hadron Collider, 93
Leap seconds, 77
Leibnitz, Gottfried, 110, 122
Leucippus, 138
'Life', Game of, 125-6, 127
Light, 91, 132
" speed of, 82, 120, 133

Light cones, 83
Limbic system, 106,
Lincoln, Abraham, 15-16, 41
Linhares (Brazil), 14
Lodge, Oliver, 66
Logarithm tables, 110
Loop quantum gravity (LQG), 95-6, 133, 134
Lorber, John, 40, 110, 114, 128
Lucid dreaming (*see* Dreams – lucid)

McAuliffe, Christa, 48
Magnetism, 52, 104, 132
Manifestation, 149-50, 152
Manifold (26-dimensional), 157
Marconi, Guglielmo, 130
Marie Antoinette, 12
Marine, Donna, 31
Mars, 57, 164
Martinique, 18-19
Marx, Karl, 139
Mass, 82, 133, 134
Mathematics, 115-27
    " laws of, 149, 152, 173
'Maverick' scientists, 129-31
Meditation, 50, 86
Mediums, 54-5
Medulla oblongata, 25
Memory, 108, 154, 169-70
Mental body (*see* Body, Mental)
Mercury (planet), 61, 164
Meta-analysis, 73
Michelson-Morley experiment,

82, 90
Midbrain, 107
Miinehoma, 48-9
Mill, John Stuart, 139
Mind, 171
Minnesota, 48
Moberley, Anne, 10-12
Modulo arithmetic, 116
Momentum, 92, 119
    " angular, 119
Monroe, Marylin, 42
Monroe, Robert, 25-7, 38, 104
Montélimar, 13, 143, 170
Moody, Raymond, 28-30
Moon, 57, 76, 164
    " 'void of course', 64
M-theory, 95, 133
Muldoon, Sylvan, 23-5, 38, 104
Multiverse, 99
Musical scales, 118
Myelin sheath, 103
Myers-Briggs profiles, 162
Myers, Frederic, 66, 67

Napier's bones, 110
Naseby, Battle of, 10
Near-death experiences, 27-30
Nelson, John, 60
Neptune, 60, 61, 159
Neurons, 102-4
Neutrinos, 94
Neutrons, 94
Newcastle upon Tyne, 42, 53
Newton, Isaac, 65, 122

Norfolk, 38
Nothing, 145-6, 149, 152, 172
'Now', 76, 85-6
Numbers, 115-8, 140

Observer, 76, 93, 100, 135, 149-50, 152, 167, 172
" point, 167
Occam's razor, 81, 149, 150
Ogston, Alexander, 27-8
O'Hare Airport, 17-18
Olfactory bulbs, 106
Out-of-body experiences, 21, 23-7
Oxford, 42, 47, 170

Pacific Ocean, 49
Parallel universes, 98-9
Parker, Adrian, 70
Parmenides, 146
Particles:
" elementary, 91-2, 93-5, 132, 134
" virtual, 133
Pascal, Blaise, 110
Peer review, 129
Pelée, Mount, 18-19
Pendulum:
" clock, 77
" dowsing, 53-4
Penrose, Roger, 80
'Persona', 167, 171
Philosophy, 138-44
" political, 139

Photons, 91, 132
Pi (π), 117
Pike (fish), 8
Pinboard experiment, 124
Pineal body, 107
Piper Alpha disaster, 48
Planck, Max, 85, 90-1, 130-1
" constant (*h*), 85, 91, 120
" length, 85, 156
" time, 85, 156
Planets, 159, 163-4
Plant life, 168
Plate tectonics, 6
Plato, 129
Playfair, Guy Lyon, 32
Pliny the Elder, 6
Pons, 107
Potassium ions, 103
Precession of the equinoxes, 63, 163
Precognition, 67-8
Precognition-remote perception (PRP), 69
Probability, 67-9, 121
Programming, 110-2
" heuristic, 112
Protons, 94
Psychical Research, Society for (SPR) (*see* Society for ...)
Psychokinesis, 67
Puthoff, Harold, 21, 22, 70
Pye, Mr & Mrs Clifford, 12
Pythagoras, 138

Qualia113

Quantum theory, 85, 90-100, 133

Quarks, 94

Radin, Dean, 65, 73

Ramos, Jorge, 14-15

Randi, James, 66

Randles, Jenny, 13

Rank-order judging, 69

Ra Uru Hu (see Krakower, Alan)

Reader's Digest magazine, 47

Reagan, Ronald, 59

Reality, 135, 142-4

" levels, 143-4

Regulus, 63

Reincarnation, 30-4, 49-50

Relativity:

" general, 84, 159

" special, 82-4

Remote viewing, 21, 50-1, 67

Reptilian brain (see Brain – reptilian)

Reticular formation, 109

Rhine, JB, 67

Riemann, Bernhard, 121

Ritchie, George, 29-30

Robertson, Morgan, 16-17, 151

Robots (see Artificial intelligence)

Rollright Stones, 54

Roman Catholic Church, 130

r-Pentomino, 126

Russell, Bertrand, 139

Russia, 20

St Pierre (Martinique), 18-19

Sakharov, Andrei, 84, 95-6

Sanderson, Ivan T, 131

San Francisco, 60-1, 159

Saturn, 57, 58, 60, 163

Scientific approach, 1-3, 174

Schrödinger, Erwin, 92-3

" cat, 92-3

" equation, 93

Scole experiment, 38-40

Scriptural approach, 1-3, 174

Séances, 38, 53-4

Sea urchins, 118

Second law of thermodynamics, 78, 81, 128-9

Shamanic approach, 1-3, 174

Self v not-self, 152

Sheldrake, Rupert, 131

Sheffield University, 40

Sherman, Harold, 22-3

Sibelius, Jean, 140

Simultaneity, 83, 150

Singh, Titu, 32

Singularity, 86-7

Sirius, 76

Slide rule, 110

Smith, Adam, 139

Society for Psychical Research (SPR), 39, 66

Socrates, 129

Sodium ions, 103

Software packages, 112
Solomon, Grant & Jane, 39
Soul, 169-70, 171
Space, 153
" 'e/m', 154, 155
" 'manifest', 156
" pixellated, 63-4, 84, 96-7, 159-60, 165
" 'spatial', 153, 155
" 'temporal', 153, 155
" 'transcendent', 154, 156
Spacetime, 83, 97, 134
Speed of light (see Light, Speed of)
Spin, 92
Spirit, 170, 171
Split-brain operation, 105
Standard deviation (σ), 71-2
Standard model, 93-4, 132
Stanford Research Institute (SRI), 70
Starfish, 118
Statistics, 71-4, 121
'Sterons', 157
String theory, 95
Sunspots, 60
Superposition, 92
Swann, Ingo, 21-3
Synaesthesia, 140-1

Tao Te Ching, 141
Targ, Russell, 21, 22, 70
Taurus, 57
Telepathy, 67, 170

Tesla, Nikola, 87, 130
Thalamus, 107
Thatcher, Margaret, 59
Thermodynamics (see Second law of ...)
Thermometers, 77
Time (see also Space, temporal), 76-89, 133, 153
" arrow of, 78-9
" cyclic, 80-1
" definition, 76
" dilation, 82, 84
" finite, 79
" imaginary, 80
" infinite, 79
" reality of, 88
" travel, 86-8
Time Storms, 13
Tipler, Frank, 87
" cylinder, 87
Titanic disaster, 16-17
Titor, John, 87-8
Tomorrow's World programme, 46
'Topons', 157
Totnes, 35
Transistors, 111
Trevalga, 13
Turing, Alan, 110

UFOs, 35, 143-4
Universe, 171
Uranus, 60, 61, 159

Versailles, Palace of, 10-12, 157

Vesuvius, 5-6

Vimperk, 49

Virgo, 57

Virtual particles (*see* Particles, virtual)

Viruses (biological), 168

Visual cortex, 105

Volcanoes, 5-6, 18-19, 44-5

Von Neumann, John, 110

Wadebridge, 12

Wambach, Helen, 34-5

Water molecule, 102

Wave-particle duality, 92, 134

Weather forecasting, 121, 124

Wegener, Alfred, 6

Wernicke's area, 104

Wheeler, John, 88

Wheeler-De Witt equation, 88

Whitehead, Alfred North, 139

Whitley Bay, 42

Witten, Edward, 95

Wittmann, Marc, 86

Wormholes, 87

X-rays, 132

Ythan (river), 8

Zener cards, 67-8

Zeno's paradox, 147

Zero, 118

Zodiac signs, 56-7, 160-2

Zytglogge (clock), 142

6th Books investigates the paranormal, supernatural, explainable or unexplainable. Titles cover everything included within parapsychology: how to, lifestyles, beliefs, myths, theories and memoir.